Renovating Your Writing

Renovating Your Writing outlines the principles of effective composition by focusing on the essential skill set and mindset every successful writer must possess. Now in its second edition, this novel text provides readers with unique strategies for crafting and revising their writing, whether for school, work, or play. The new edition emphasizes, in particular, the importance of the writer embracing a rhetorical perspective, distinguishing between formal and social media compositional styles, and appreciating the effort needed to produce clear, concise, and compelling messages.

Richard Kallan chairs the Communication Department at California State Polytechnic University, Pomona. He has taught writing at several colleges, including the University of Southern California (USC Marshall School of Business) and the University of California, Santa Barbara (Writing Program). Over the years, he has instructed courses spanning four disciplines: communication studies, journalism, English, and business.

Renovating Your Writing

Shaping Ideas and Arguments
into Clear, Concise, and Compelling
Messages

2nd edition

Richard Kallan

Routledge
Taylor & Francis Group

NEW YORK AND LONDON

Second edition published 2018
by Routledge
711 Third Avenue, New York, NY 10017

and by Routledge
2 Park Square, Milton Park, Abingdon, Oxon, OX14 4RN

Routledge is an imprint of the Taylor & Francis Group, an informa business

© 2018 Taylor & Francis

First published by Pearson 2012

Library of Congress Cataloging in Publication Data
Names: Kallan, Richard A., 1948- author.
Title: Renovating your writing : shaping ideas and arguments into clear, concise and compelling messages / Richard Kallan.
Description: Second edition. | New York, NY, Milton Park, Abingdon, Oxon : Routledge, [2017]
Identifiers: LCCN 2017001583| ISBN 9781138726765 (hardback) | ISBN 9781138726772 (pbk.) | ISBN 9781315186603 (ebk.)
Subjects: LCSH: English language—Rhetoric. | Composition (Language arts)
Classification: LCC PE1408 .K257 2017 | DDC 808/.042–dc23
LC record available at https://lccn.loc.gov/2017001583

ISBN: 978-1-138-72676-5 (hbk)
ISBN: 978-1-138-72677-2 (pbk)
ISBN: 978-1-315-18660-3 (ebk)

Typeset in Optima
by Florence Production Ltd, Stoodleigh, Devon, UK

Visit the companion website: www.routledge.com/cw/kallan

For Daniel Kallan, my father, and Jerry Novotny, my high school newspaper advisor, who took turns teaching me how to write a *sentence*; and Robert D. Brooks, director of my master's thesis, who showed me how to craft a *paragraph*. Guided by the lessons of these mentors, I am still working on the *page*.

Contents

Acknowledgments

Readers familiar with the first edition of *Renovating Your Writing* will notice several significant changes in this second edition. I have added, deleted, restructured, and revised material in an effort to sharpen the book's focus and applicability. This newer text benefited substantially from the close reading and insightful suggestions of Darla Anderson, Cristina Fucaloro, Jerald Goldstein, Tina McCorkindale, Rebecca Mills, and Wayne Rowe. I also remain indebted to Jeffrey Brand, Daniel R. Fredrick, Patricia S. Hill, Lawrence A. Hosman, John Levine, Daryle Nagano, and Esther Rumsey for their earlier reviews of the original manuscript.

Note on Text

Some portions of this book originally appeared in Robert Gunning and Richard Kallan, *How to Take the Fog Out of Business Writing*, Dartnell, 1994; Richard Kallan, "Teaching Journalistic Cogency with 55-Word Short Stories," *Journalism & Mass Communication Educator*, vol. 55, no 3, 2000, adapted with permission; and Richard Kallan, "Thoughts on Right Way to Write" and "Weigh Letter of Application Carefully," guest columns, published concurrently in *Pasadena Star-News, San Gabriel Valley Tribune*, and *Whittier Daily News*, May 12, 2008, and May 19, 2008.

Introduction

Achieving Proficiency in Writing

The power of language to move audiences and effect change is profound. Sometimes the impact is immediate and dramatic, as seen in iconic examples of great literature and sterling oratory. More often, it occurs over time: any well-crafted written message, regardless of its purpose, ultimately functions to inform audience values and beliefs, which, in turn, shape audience attitudes and behaviors. The more skilled you become as a writer, the greater your ability to extend your influence by fashioning messages appropriate for any writing situation, no matter how unique and demanding.

But it is not just *audiences* that are transformed by the written word. The process of trying to create a clear, concise, and compelling message also changes you, *the writer*, because it invites continual evaluation of the strengths and weaknesses of your message and, correspondingly, ongoing evaluation of your values, your beliefs, and your larger worldview. Such self-examination and self-critique fosters exploration and discovery of what you want to say and why, and how best to say it with confidence and conviction. Too, the writing process functions to enhance the development and expression of critical thinking skills that can be applied to other, non-writing venues, including public speaking, interpersonal communication, and group participation.

Additionally, the better you write, the better you read; you become more adept at decoding messages and analyzing how they function. And, of course, the ability to write well also leads to greater success in the classroom, in the job market, and in any setting that features written expression.

Despite the enormous importance of writing and its championing by nearly everyone, proficiency in writing remains an elusive goal for many. Ill-conceived, badly executed writing appears everywhere. Consider these common scenarios:

- A ponderous report about how to improve campus parking is set aside because it is unreadable, resulting in vital information being ignored.
- An imprecise e-mail to a classmate working on a group project spurs the opposite action intended, wasting time and misdirecting the group's focus.
- An unclear letter to an employer is so confusing that it requires another letter to correct its mistakes, leading to more work and a potentially strained relationship.
- A poorly organized term paper casts the author as less knowledgeable than in actuality.

First-year college students often require remedial writing instruction, and while several will graduate with improved writing skills, far fewer will become accomplished writers. Why is proficiency in writing so difficult for so many people? Why does the challenge persist well after we have all been repeatedly schooled in the process? Why don't the lessons always "stick" even when imparted by the best teachers using the latest (and supposedly best) pedagogy/textbooks on the subject?

Perhaps the problem is that too often writing instruction fails to set forth guidelines that are both practical and nuanced; absent are layered lessons that can be adapted to a host of different writing situations. *Renovating Your Writing* offers an antidote by providing a compact tutorial *and* an extended exploration of the essential macro and micro tasks every successful writer must perform to enhance the processing and appeal of his/her message. It veers away from trying to discuss the whole of composition, an approach that implicitly bestows equal importance on all that is covered and comes at the expense of treating key topics less comprehensively. In contrast, *Renovating Your Writing* mines a somewhat narrower field in an effort to more thoroughly examine the core *skill set* and *mindset* central to the writing process. It is not an entry-level, beginner's book with coverage of such topics as how to choose a subject, access databases and research tools, and evaluate information. Instead, it is aimed at those more experienced in expressing themselves who want to take their writing to the next level both in the classroom and in the workplace. The strategies, tactics, and tips it presents serve as a blueprint for self-revising your writing into clear, concise, and compelling messages.

Rethinking Your Thoughts about Writing

Most writing instruction fails to acknowledge the teaching and learning challenges that spring from various misperceptions many of us have about writing in general and our own writing in particular.

Many of us think we write better than we do. Academics, of course, lead the pack. Even when they pen something they admit is arduous to follow, it is never because of *how* it is written. Rather it is because the ideas expressed are so profound they could not possibly have been expressed in any other way. For some, clear and concise writing signals the work of a lesser mind that entertains simpler ideas. Complex thought does invite a more complex syntactical structure, but the text must remain readable.

Although academics would top the rankings in any national poll of authorial self-esteem, they are not alone. Most of us misjudge our writing abilities and not because we are delusional or egomaniacal.

When we write, we regularly omit many of the sense-making connectives—background information, key explanation, helpful transitions, and supportive logic—vital to creating a text that makes us sound rational. Instead, we "subvocalize" (mentally fill in) these missing links as we write and review our text. Our writing, thus, makes sense to us, and often only to us, because we read it in a way no one else does.

To know what it is like to be your reader, take a sample of your best writing and set it aside for several months, long enough to forget the sense-making connectives that swirled in your head at the time you were composing, but which never made it into the final paper. Without the benefit of this additional, unwritten text to guide you, now reread what you wrote. Experiencing your writing this way, in much the same way as would your audience, is eye-opening and humbling. Your formerly eloquent words probably do not seem quite as refined as you first thought. Yes, it is easy to overestimate the quality of your writing.

Unfortunately, setting aside a writing assignment for long stretches between edits is not usually practical, especially if you hope to graduate. (To the rescue, Chapter 5 offers a helpful tool to immediately gauge the readability of your writing.)

Many of us think we can develop our writing skills with less time and effort than necessary. Nearly everyone acknowledges the importance of writing well, and nearly everyone says that writing takes time and effort. But most of us still underestimate just how much time and effort are required. Although some writers can compose quickly and eloquently, the process usually proves labor intensive, particularly for conscientious writers trying to meet their own threshold of excellence. The stellar writing they seek is hallmarked by two characteristics:

- It exudes a distinct sound, an unmistakable rhythm and grace. The writer embraces metaphor as well as other figures of speech and commands a polished syntax that flows so smoothly one can read it aloud quickly without ever stumbling over awkward phrasing. It is the kind of writing found in such magazines as *The New Yorker*, *Esquire*, *The Atlantic*, *Vanity Fair*, and *Rolling Stone*.

- It exhibits impeccable structure, which, next to rhythm and grace, may well be the toughest element of writing to master. A text rich in content can be especially difficult to structure into a unified and coherent whole where similar ideas come together seamlessly. Even exceptional writers struggle with organization, their eloquence suffering when it is subverted by maverick sentences allowed to roam about untethered to main ideas or main arguments. Orchestrating an orderly, soundly sequenced progression of thoughts is never easy.

Outstanding writing skills can take a lifetime to develop, and, still, many will never achieve the goal. Thankfully, most writing required of school, work, and home needs "only" to be clear, concise, and compelling.

Many of us think—because we have been told so many times—we can significantly improve our writing skills by simply reading more and writing more. After all, isn't that what every teacher has told us since day one? Under the right conditions, reading more and writing more can improve writing skills, but neither activity by itself will transform your writing.

First, it is *what* you read and *how* you read that counts. Great literature can enlighten and inspire, as well as instill a love of language and all that it is capable of communicating. But simply devouring fiction (novels, plays, poetry), whose purpose, structure, and style differ so markedly from non-fiction (term papers, essays, reports, letters, memos), will not teach you specifically about nonfiction writing. If it did, every voracious reader of such literature would be a great writer. All are not, and, in fact, many do not seem to write much better than their literature-light counterparts. Nor will your writing improve by simply reading a lot of nonfiction—unless you choose quality nonfiction, and then, as you read, closely analyze the text in terms of the choices the author makes. Seldom does this happen.

Second, you will not become a better writer just by writing more. One need only survey the millions of blogs faithfully produced every day to realize that practice alone does not make perfect. It is the informed practice of *rewriting*, not just the act of composing, that improves writing skills. Lest you approach writing unprepared for its demands, you must first know the principles of effective composition and then engage in constant revision. In this way, writing is like any other accomplished skill: it is the product of knowledge, sustained practice, and ongoing self-evaluation and self-correction.

As you become a better writer, you may be surprised to learn that you are not also becoming a faster writer. Ironically, writing speed typically decreases with improved skills because now better able to recognize and appreciate quality writing you set higher standards for yourself. Additionally, the ease with which computers allow for rewriting slows the process given it is so easy to keep revising and improving drafts.

Many of us think our writing will be carefully read by an *ideal* audience. Expecting readers to eagerly await our every word, we create texts as if our audience were our adoring mom and dad, or perhaps our loving spouse or partner. We write for a perfectly attentive, perfectly perceptive, perfectly analytic audience . . . an audience that rarely exists. More often, our readers are short on time and patience; overwhelmed with information, much of which they would prefer not to read; and used to skipping and skimming nearly everything they read. They are not our mom and dad.

A better perspective, even when you know otherwise, is to assume your reader is tired and cranky, bored by your subject, opposed to your position, and hostile toward you. When you write for this less-than-ideal reader, you are forced to focus on what is most important: getting the audience to read, understand, and accept your message. You lead with your best ideas and arguments, develop them more efficiently, and refrain from off-handed comments that usually are not all that clever or relevant. You stay more earnest, less apt to come across as cocky, boorish, or overbearing.

Readers can never be taken for granted; they must continually be courted. As such, it is important to realize that all writing is persuasive in three distinct ways.

The writer first attempts to convince the potential audience to read what is written. Documents visually inviting—easier and more interesting to read owing to their attractive layout and formatting—are more likely to summon the audience's attention. Whether they continue to hold that attention, and to what extent, is a matter of readability: how clearly, concisely, and compellingly the message comes across. Seen in this context, your writing must function foremost to secure and maintain your readers' attention.

When we say that all writing is persuasive, we also mean that all writing seeks to persuade its readers to believe and act upon what they read. Even the most descriptive of messages is persuasive: the writer tries to convince the reader to accept the presented information as believable. The difference between asking your audience to vote for a specific candidate and describing the voting process is one of degree more than kind. In both cases, the writer's primary task is to present credible arguments or descriptions the reader can trust. In the former example, the call to action is explicit, while in the latter it is implicit insofar as beliefs lead to corollary behaviors. In other words, knowing about the voting process leads one to be more willing or less willing to vote. In both cases, your perceived trustworthiness, wrought by everything you do as a writer, is central to your persuasibility. Always, readers must come to trust you if they are to believe what you are saying. In both personal writing and formal expression, credible ideas/ arguments increase your persuasibility and the chances your audience will accept your message.

Finally, all writing functions persuasively and sometimes in unintended ways. In large measure, this is because all language carries both denotative and connotative meaning. *Denotative* refers to what a word commonly signifies; it is the literal dictionary definition that describes a word's usage. *Connotative* refers to the subjective or implied meaning we associate with words based on our personal experience with what they reference. The denotative meaning of ice cream, for example, is a cold, soft-textured, sweet dessert. Its connotative meaning, for most people, is an enjoyable, often socially anchored, experience tied to positive memories.

Because words do not hold identical connotative meanings for everyone, the meanings they elicit differ. Hence, it becomes impossible to create a wholly neutral message whose meaning and impact are the same for all audiences. Words conjure up unique audience experiences, positive and negative, which affect the processing and appeal of every message. To think otherwise is to be misguided by what I.A. Richards in *The Philosophy of Rhetoric* refers to as the "Proper Meaning Superstition," which is the belief "that a word has a meaning of its own (ideally, only one) independent of and controlling its use and the purpose for which it should be uttered."[1]

If neutral-languaged messages could somehow be produced, they would still function persuasively. Even those meant only to describe, report, or explain would *both* inform and persuade. What we know molds our values and beliefs, which then shapes our attitudes and behaviors. Knowing that violent crime is increasing in your neighborhood could convince you that more gun ownership is needed, or, conversely, that greater gun control should be enacted. This helps explain why authorial intent and message function are not always congruent. Shepherded by the writer, the reader "completes" the meaning of the message, but not without bringing along his/her own sense-making experience that contributes to the message's persuasive potential.

To be sure, writers must embrace a *rhetorical* perspective that views every compositional choice they make as affecting the processing and appeal of their message, and approaches all writing as strategically and functionally persuasive. It is a perspective that mirrors Aristotle's definition of *rhetoric*: "an ability, in each [particular] case, to see the available means of persuasion."[2] Persuasion itself is neither inherently sinister nor manipulative; its aims and means are products of each writer's moral sensibility.

Many of us think we dislike writing. Students, in particular, often say they hate writing, even to the extent of wanting to avoid courses having substantial writing assignments. Yet these same students find no such displeasure in voraciously texting, tweeting, Facebooking, blogging, and participating in other kinds of social media messaging. Certainly, it is not writing per se that students abhor.

Students enjoy communicating what is interesting and important to them as opposed to what may be interesting and important to someone else (such as their teachers). Highly informal, "personal" writing is favored over more structured, "formal" expression, such as academic and workplace writing, because the subject matter holds greater relevance for students. Too, the message can be executed without readers expecting the writer to faithfully follow the principles of standard composition—although, ironically, the lack of such knowledge limits technical creativity, leading to missed opportunities for more effective expression. Nevertheless, personal and formal writing do share key similarities; understanding one can inform and improve the practice of the other.

This is not to say that formal writing should mirror personal writing or vice versa. Each form serves a very different audience and communication function. Formal writing does not allow for the "shorthand" communication style that personal writing affords, whereby the reader can infer meaning and make contextual sense of highly abbreviated content owing to the reader and writer's shared experiences. Moreover, formal writing, compared to personal writing, addresses subject matter whose audiences expect greater message development in the form of detail, qualification, and support. Writing formal messages is more complicated to the extent it calls for more complex and nuanced syntax, leading to longer and more layered sentence structures.

A series of social media postings obviously differs from a term paper, but the best of both feature three transcending qualities: (1) The message is easily accessible; (2) the message is economically expressed; and (3) the message effects a desired reader response. *Renovating Your Writing* focuses on the skill set and mindset needed to secure these qualities and produce writing that is clear, concise, and compelling.

Structure of the Book

Unlike beginning composition books organized *top-down*, usually starting with how to choose a topic and develop a thesis before moving on to sentence structure and word choice, *Renovating Your Writing* is organized *ground-up*, starting with how to write and revise sentences, before proceeding to paragraphs and pages. This approach reflects the view that the art of renovating your writing must begin with a firm understanding of the basic units of composition.

Part I, "Strategies, Tactics, and Tips," explores the crafting of sentences, paragraphs, and pages. Chapter 1 focuses on ways to build clear, concise, and compelling sentences that express your meaning; Chapter 2 details how to forge unified and coherent paragraphs and pages to ensure maximum accessibility and impact; Chapter 3 further expounds on strategies, tactics, and tips for producing a unique and relevant, audience-engaging text that strategically carries forth your ideas and arguments; and Chapter 4 shows how to drive home your message visually, as well as how to revise your writing in new and inventive ways.

Part II, "Additional Tools," includes Chapter 5, a guide for easily and quickly determining the readability of your writing; and Chapter 6, a creative writing exercise designed to help you develop a more cogent style.

The pages that follow often allude to the writer's need to make fine distinctions. Why should one fret over details when larger issues—like developing, structuring, and supporting a thesis—lurk around the bend? Isn't it a luxury to discuss word choice, for example, in the context of the seemingly more substantive tasks you must complete to create a well-written paper? An attention to detail—*not* an immobilizing obsession—is important because it is the starting point for approaching *every* aspect of your writing. More than just a step you carry out in the post-production process of your writing, an attention to detail mirrors a larger, holistic perspective that informs all your critical thinking and expression. This mindset coupled with a corresponding skill set enables you to produce clear, concise, and compelling writing.

Renovation Tip

It helps to "rest" your writing. The next time you finish an important assignment, consider it *almost* done. Put it down, walk away, and work on something else for a while. Then return to the assignment and read it as if you are seeing it for the first time; pretend you are the reader. This will allow you to spot the little cracks that cause your reader to stumble, as well as the larger ruptures that can level entire understanding. Although you can catch many problems by reading over your message carefully, it becomes more difficult to see all the flaws as you get closer to your writing. The longer your writing "rests" between rewritings, the easier it becomes to "distance" yourself from your writing and read it afresh.

Notes

1   Richards, I. A. *The Philosophy of Rhetoric.* Oxford University Press, 1965, p. 11.

2   Aristotle. *Aristotle on Rhetoric: A Theory of Civic Discourse.* Translated by George A. Kennedy, Oxford University Press, 1991, p. 36.

I

Strategies, Tactics, and Tips

Constructing Sentences

When you write, it helps to envision yourself as a verbal architect charged with creatively using all the materials (words) at your disposal to build structures, ascending in size (sentences, paragraphs, and pages). Like all good architectural works, these structures should function effectively and efficiently, while exhibiting a pleasing aesthetic inviting to visitors. You must design and construct sentences that are clear, concise, and compelling.

Let's start with what is meant by a sentence.

Distinguishing between Complete and Incomplete Sentences

To know what constitutes a sentence is to understand the terms commonly used to express its defining characteristics.

A complete sentence features one or more independent clauses. An **independent clause** is a related word grouping that can stand alone as a sentence because it (1) includes a subject and a predicate and (2) expresses a complete thought.

The **subject** is the who or what that initiates or receives whatever is happening in the sentence. The **predicate** describes the happening; it commences with a **verb**, which most often is an action.

I [subject] enjoy [verb] my writing class.
enjoy my writing class = the predicate

Other times, the verb establishes a *condition* by serving as a **linking verb** that, in essence, functions much like an equal sign to connect the subject and the condition.

<u>Writing</u> [subject] <u>is</u> [linking verb] <u>fun</u> [condition].
<u>is fun</u> = the predicate

Occasionally, the subject of a sentence is implied.

Run! (The implied subject of the command is you.)
<u>Run</u> = the predicate

The predicate comprises the verb and usually one or more of the following:

- a **direct object**—the recipient of the verb's action;
- an **indirect object**—the recipient to whom or for whom the action was intended;
- a **complement**—one or more words that essentially either (a) renames the subject or the direct object or (b) describes the subject or the direct object; and
- **modifiers**—one or more words that modify the verb portion of the predicate. Words and word groupings that modify verbs usually take the form of adverbs, adverbial clauses, and prepositional phrases (reviewed in Box 1.1).

Sometimes, the predicate includes only a verb. A verb-only predicate is possible when the sentence features an **intransitive verb**—a verb that requires no object or complement to complete the thought and form a complete sentence. For example: *He died. I cried. She celebrated.* (*Died, cried,* and *celebrated* are intransitive verbs.) A **transitive verb**, on the other hand, requires a direct object to complete the thought.

<u>Lucy</u> [subject] <u>bought</u> [transitive verb] <u>a composition book</u> [direct object].

<u>Lucy</u> [subject] <u>loaned</u> [transitive verb] <u>Hazyl</u> [indirect object] <u>her composition book</u> [direct object].

Box 1.1 Common Verb Modifiers

Adverb. A word that modifies a verb, an adjective, or another adverb. When an adverb modifies a verb, it describes when, where, why, how, how often/to what degree, and under what conditions the action/condition occurred. *I quickly [adverb] wrote [verb] three papers.* When an adverb modifies either an adjective or another adverb, it embellishes or elaborates upon the adjective or adverb. *I wrote an extremely [adverb] long [adjective] paper. I wrote this paper extremely [adverb] quickly [adverb].* (Note: An **adjective** is a word that describes a noun or a pronoun by qualifying or quantifying it. A **noun** names a person, place, thing, activity, quality, or concept; a **pronoun** refers to, or replaces, a noun.)

Adverbial clause. A dependent clause that functions as an adverb. *I submitted my paper before I realized it was for the wrong class [adverbial clause]. I included 134 footnotes in my paper because I thought it would help my grade [adverbial clause].*

Prepositional phrase. A modifying phrase beginning with a preposition (a word such as *above, across, around, at, behind, below, between, by, down, from, in, of, on, onto, out, over, since, to, through, toward, up, with,* and *within*) that normally functions as an adjective or adverb. *My paper comprised Facebook evidence of the highest quality [prepositional phrase functioning as an adjective]. I wrote my paper on my way to class [prepositional phrase functioning as an adverb].*

More examples of subjects with predicates:

- The plural of ellipsis [subject] is [linking verb] ellipses [complement that renames the subject; also known as a **predicate noun**].

- Punctuation [subject] is [linking verb] easy [complement that describes the subject; also known as a **predicate adjective**].

15

- She [subject] <u>considered</u> [transitive verb] <u>fine literature</u> [direct object] <u>her salvation</u> [complement that renames the direct object].

- He [subject] <u>found</u> [transitive verb] <u>his 6th-grade grammar book</u> [direct object] <u>dusty and dog-eared</u> [complement that describes the direct object].

- He [subject] <u>footnoted</u> [transitive verb] <u>his paper</u> [direct object] <u>carefully</u> [adverbial modifier].

- She [subject] <u>completed</u> [transitive verb] <u>her research</u> [direct object] <u>in the old campus library</u> [prepositional phrase modifier].

Along with having a subject and a predicate, a complete sentence expresses a *complete thought*: a "finished" declaration, exclamation/command, or question. Note how these sentences have a subject and a predicate but remain incomplete:

- Although I love to write.
- When class starts.
- If I may ask.

Each sentence is incomplete because the writer begins but never finishes the larger thought the sentence structure promises. Instead, we have three dependent (or subordinate) clauses. A **dependent** (or **subordinate**) **clause** contains a subject and a predicate, but it does not express a complete thought. Unable to stand alone, a dependent clause must precede or follow an independent clause to form a complete sentence. Dependent clauses are introduced with **subordinating conjunctions**, such as *after, although, because, before, how, if, provided (that), since, supposing, unless, until, when, whether, wherever, while.*

Incomplete sentence: Although I love to write.

Complete sentence: Although I love to write, I don't always get good grades on my papers.

Complete sentence: I don't always get good grades on my papers, although I love to write.

(Sometimes, as in this example, the dependent clause can be revised into a complete, albeit narrower-meaning, sentence by simply eliminating the subordinating word. Dependent clause: *Although I love to write.* Independent clause: *I love to write.*)

Incomplete sentence:	When class starts.
Complete sentence:	When class starts, students must be present and prepared!
Complete sentence:	Students must be present and prepared when class starts!
Incomplete sentence:	If I may ask.
Complete sentence:	If I may ask, how did you learn to write so well?
Complete sentence:	How did you learn to write so well, if I may ask?

An incomplete sentence (also referred to as a **sentence fragment**) takes the form of either a dependent clause; a **phrase**, which is a related word grouping that does not have a subject and a predicate; or a single (non-command) word. *Because those are the rules. Alright, readers, any quest-ions? Good.*

We often talk in incomplete sentences. This explains their prevalence in written dialogue, where authors try to capture the way people actually converse.

"The way people really talk?"
"Yes, the way people talk."
"Everyone?"
"Yup!"
"Even authors of books on writing?"
"Yes, even them."

Incomplete sentences abound in personal forms of writing, whose sound and structure reflect how we talk. For writers and readers in a hurry, the incomplete sentence also proves quicker to compose and, usually, to process. Still, the incomplete sentence can be problematic when it hampers the audience's understanding of what the writer wants to say. Take this example:

17

He did not pass the test, although he studied a lot. While he was watching television and pondering his future. He came to realize it would have been helpful to have bought the text for the course.

Did he study a lot while watching television and pondering his future? Or did he realize while watching television and pondering his future that he should have bought the text? *While he was watching television and pondering his future* is an incomplete sentence, a dependent clause needing to be attached to the sentence that precedes or follows it. When that happens, the meaning is clear.

He did not pass the test, although he studied a lot while he was watching television and pondering his future.

Or

While he was watching television and pondering his future, he came to realize it would have been helpful to have bought the text for the course.

Used occasionally and knowingly in more formal documents, the incomplete sentence is fine. But the *unintended* incomplete sentence, which sophisticated readers will recognize, can lower your credibility and stamp you as a novice.

When would it be appropriate to write an incomplete sentence in more formal prose?

Here are two instances:

1. When you list entries or items following an introductory-type sentence (as just demonstrated).

2. When an incomplete sentence best expresses or emphasizes your thought (**bolded** = incomplete sentence).

    Sixteen. The number of times the writer resorts to beginning a sentence with "suddenly." Mind you, just in the first chapter. Is this author worth reading? **Probably not.**

And from the Pulitzer-prize winning columnist Mary McNamara's review of the HBO series *The Night Of:*

Though incapable of many things that make the modern man, Stone [the main character] still loves. **His son, his job, his notion of justice, even the cat the murdered girl has left behind.**

And because he loves, Stone still hopes. **Reluctantly, secretly and, perhaps, in vain but enough to keep moving forward.**

Which is the great act of heroism an anti-antihero can achieve.[1]

Even when employed effectively, however, the breezy informality of the incomplete sentence cautions against its overuse.

Renovation Tip

Many writers tend to structure all their sentences the same way: they begin with the subject followed by the predicate. *I* [subject] *enjoy reading a graceful sentence* [predicate]. *This paragraph* [subject] *is boring* [predicate]. *Poorly written sentences* [subject] *make me sad* [predicate].

Repetitive use of the subject–predicate formula becomes stale quickly. To vary your sentence structure and create a more engaging reading experience, think of how you might write your typical subject–predicate sentence differently without it sounding awkward or odd. Rather than *I enjoy reading a graceful sentence*, consider alternatives, such as:

- *Reading a graceful sentence* [subject] *brings me great enjoyment* [predicate].

- *One of my greatest enjoyments* [subject] *is reading a graceful sentence* [predicate].

Breaking the tedium of repetitive sentence structure is not difficult. Words can be moved about in various ways to freshen your style and to emphasize one thought over another. Once you see the need for variation, you will have no problem finding new ways to write sentences. You might even pose a rhetorical question (a dramatic question to which everyone knows the answer) to drive home your

continued

idea or argument. *After all, wouldn't you want to use every possible tool to enhance your persuasibility? And would any reader ever object to a sentence style richer and more varied?*

Even good writers can be overly cautious, if not staid, in their sentence construction. Afraid of making a mistake, they stick to conventional, syntactically safe constructions devoid of any personality, let alone stylishness. It is better to take creative chances from time to time and risk occasionally breaking a rule of grammar, punctuation, usage, or mechanics than to always settle for sentences that come across as bland and colorless.

Balancing the Demands of a Sentence

A sentence should be clear, concise, and compelling. These qualities overlap, intersect, and sometimes compete. Conciseness usually results in greater clarity because it strips away unnecessary and misdirecting verbiage; correspondingly, the desire to achieve clarity often induces conciseness. However, many a writer trying to be clear resorts to repetition, and many a writer trying to be concise omits clarifying information. Adding to the challenge of writing clear and concise sentences is the need to be compelling. A compelling sentence sufficiently and credibly details its main thought; it does not abridge or oversimplify its wholeness in the name of conciseness. Lest we forget, Stanley Fish reminds us in *How to Write a Sentence and How to Read One*, "People write or speak sentences in order to produce an effect, and the success of a sentence is measured by the degree to which the desired effect has been achieved."[2]

Reinhold Niebuhr's Serenity Prayer, widely adopted by various 12-Step Recovery Groups, most notably Alcoholics Anonymous, offers a good example of how clear, concise, and compelling thoughts come together to form a poignant sentence.

God grant me the serenity
to accept the things I cannot change;
courage to change the things I can;
and wisdom to know the difference.

Interestingly, this popular version of the Serenity Prayer followed Niebuhr's original, slightly longer version.

> God, give me grace to accept with serenity
> the things that cannot be changed,
> courage to change the things
> which should be changed,
> and the wisdom to distinguish
> the one from the other.

Which do **you** prefer? Does the additional language in the original version add to the Serenity Prayer's meaning and impact, or can it be deleted beneficially?

When you are unclear and inconcise, you obscure your point of view, rendering it less readable and less appealing. For many of us, the problem emerges when we write more formally, and it increases proportionally as that formality rises. How, then, can we write formal, compelling sentences that are still clear and concise? What can the process of personal writing teach us that might help?

Because of the nature of the topics addressed, formal writing requires greater precision than does personal writing. Yet in terms of lucidity and economy (compellingness aside), it is personal writing that is usually more cogent. This comes about because of the sheer frequency and speed of personal communication in a digital age. Continually, we are asked to respond quickly to text messages, tweets, e-mails, and the like. Constraints of time and space mitigate against convoluted, verbose writing. Personal writing requires that we focus on the essential, communicating with what Jacques Barzun would say is the kind of simplicity and directness that facilitates message production and message processing.[3] In contrast, the pace and length of formal writing neither demand nor encourage simplicity or directness.

Murky sentences also result from the mindset we assume when we write formally. Prompted by the fear that everyone is watching and judging us, we want to *sound* professional, sophisticated, and intelligent. This mentality fosters a self-conscious, affected style that leads to a bloated text. We mistakenly perceive formal writing to be the antithesis of natural expression. As journalist/novelist Tom Wolfe explains:

Most people end up all of their lives doing their best writing in letters. Especially to a friend, or somebody you think understands you, and somebody you're not inhibited with, because you don't have all of those forty or fifty or seventy people looking over your shoulder that most of us feel like are there when we actually start writing for public consumption.[4]

Personal writing is much like corresponding with a friend or would-be friend. The style is simple and direct because what matters most is communicating what you want to say, rather than worrying how readers will judge your writing. Personal writing reinforces the importance of audience—even when all you are doing is talking about yourself—over self-conscious preoccupation with how the writing sounds.

The best formal writing is clear, concise, and compelling. The windy sentences that frequently typify formal writing give way to a navigable style every bit as clear and concise as personal writing, while at the same time featuring the extended message development usually absent in personal writing. Too often, however, that standard is not met by formal writing.

Below are three exemplar sentences, each followed by two alternative versions: one representing a sample of bloated writing, the other posing as a text message. Note how the confederate alternative versions fall short of capturing *all* three elements (clarity, conciseness, and compellingness) exhibited by the original.

Original: Sylvia Plath, *The Unabridged Journals of Sylvia Plath*
I want to live and feel all the shades, tones, and variations of mental and physical experience possible in my life.[5]

Bloated Version
I want to experientially embrace and emotionally encounter to the fullest extent conceivably possible the broad spectrum of mental and physical happenings, including, but not limited to, those that can be behaviorally encountered in everyday life.

Text Message Version
YOLO.

Original: Truman Capote, *In Cold Blood: A True Account of a Multiple Murder and Its Consequences*

Like the waters of the river, like the motorists on the highway, and like the yellow trains streaking down the Santa Fe tracks, drama, in the shape of exceptional happenings, had never stopped there.[6]

Bloated Version

Very much like the ever-flowing waters of the river that continually stream onward, like the motorists that can be observed driving routinely on the highway, and like the traffic patterns exhibited by yellow trains streaking hastily down the Santa Fe railroad tracks, real-world drama, operationally defined herein to mean occurrences most people would judge to be in the shape of exceptional happenings of significant rarity, had never once stopped there.

Text Message Version

Nothing crazy ever happened there B4.

Original: Umberto Eco, *The Island of the Day Before*

Absence is to love as wind to fire: it extinguishes the little flame, it fans the big.[7]

Bloated Version

The effect of absence on romantic relationships is proportionally related to the depth of those relationships, which is to say that absence will further enhance and intensify an already strong relationship; on the other hand, it will function to further diminish a relationship characterized by one or more, overriding, preexisting weaknesses.

Text Message Version

Apart 4 now. Will love grow? Depends on what we have.

As exemplified in the bloated examples, the clarity and conciseness of thought suffer when your writing is pretentious and wordy. Yet when brevity is taken to the extreme and ideational depth compromised, as seen in the text messages, a less-than-sufficient (compelling) message results. Detail, qualification, and support, when necessary, must be presented in ways that ensure clear, concise, and compelling expression.

Renovation Tip

The run-on sentence, a misstep of many beginning writers, usually takes the form of two independent clauses, one following the other, without correct punctuation separating the two. Because both thoughts run together without benefit of a pause, the sentence can be more difficult to process.

Sometimes, no punctuation comes between the two independent clauses. *The assignment did not have a page minimum or maximum we could write as long or as short as we wanted.* To fix this run-on sentence, separate the two independent clauses with either (1) a period, thereby creating two sentences; (2) a semicolon; or (3) a comma followed by a **coordinating conjunction**, of which there are seven— *for, and, nor, but, or, yet, so* (one way of remembering them is by the acronym FANBOYS).

- The assignment did not have a page minimum or maximum. We could write as short or as long as we wanted.

- The assignment did not have a page minimum or maximum; we could write as short or as long as we wanted.

- The assignment did not have a page minimum or maximum, so we could write as short or as long as we wanted.

A second type of run-on sentence, a comma splice, occurs when you use a comma to splice or join two independent clauses: *The assignment did not have a page minimum or maximum, we could write as short or as long as we wanted.* Again, the two independent clauses must be made into two sentences, or separated by a semi-colon or by a comma followed by a coordinating conjunction.

The most frequent comma splices appear when writers try to join two independent clauses using a comma followed by a **conjunctive adverb**, such as *however, consequently, hence, moreover, subsequently,* or *therefore.* For example: *I am only an average writer, however, I never write run-on sentences.* A comma followed by a conjunctive adverb cannot join two independent clauses; the sentence must be revised.

continued

> I am only an average writer. However, I never write run-on sentences.
>
> I am only an average writer; however, I never write run-on sentences.
>
> I am only an average writer, but I never write run-on sentences.
>
> You could also change the first or second independent clause to a dependent clause.
>
> Although I am only an average writer, I never write run-on sentences.
>
> I never write run-on sentences, although I am only an average writer.

Writing Clear, Concise, and Compelling Sentences

The discussion that follows focuses on the task of sentence-building. It explains why we often write the way we do and how the choices we make function, for better or worse, in communicating our message. The strategies, tactics, and tips presented stress the importance of (1) starting with active actors, (2) varying sentence length, and (3) eliminating unnecessary words.

Start with Active Actors

In an **active voice** sentence, the actor is the subject of the sentence.

- We liked our English teacher.
  We [actor and subject of the sentence] liked [active verb] our English teacher.
- College tuition increased dramatically.
  College tuition [actor and subject of the sentence] increased [active verb] dramatically.

In **passive voice**, the subject of the sentence becomes passive in the sense that it receives the action or is acted upon.

* Our English teacher was liked by us.
  Our English teacher [subject of the sentence] was liked [passive verb] by us [actor].
* College tuition was increased.
  College tuition [subject of the sentence] was increased [passive verb; no stated actor].

Active and passive verbs can be any tense.

Active Voice

Present tense:	She manages the Writer's Block Saloon.
Past tense:	She managed the Writer's Block Saloon.
Future tense:	She will manage the Writer's Block Saloon.

Passive Voice

Present tense:	The Writer's Block Saloon is managed by her.
Past tense:	The Writer's Block Saloon was managed by her.
Future tense:	The Writer's Block Saloon will be managed by her.

People rarely *talk* in passive voice. Not surprisingly, personal writing, which tends to mimic oral communication, seldom includes passive voice, whose form inverts the anticipated, customary structure of speech. The natural, conversational way to speak is in active voice: you start with the actor followed by the action. You say, *I read five books on how to write better*, not *Five books on how to write better were read by me*. Or when your aunt Rita asks whether you received the birthday gift she sent, you respond: *Yeah, I got it. Thanks!* Or should you remember she once taught English, you reply: *Yes, I received it. Thank you!* But you would never say: *Yes, your birthday gift was received by me. You are to be thanked.* On the other hand, it is common to find passive voice in formal writing, where the affected style masquerades as "proper" tone. *Your letter was received by us. The issues you raised have been discussed and evaluated by our staff. Our attempt to rectify the situation will be guided by our corporate policy, which is explained below by several more passive-voiced sentences.*

And should this not satisfy your customer, he or she might write back in kind, *It is thought by me that Hell should be gone to by you.*

Passive voice sentences are usually longer (less concise), harder to process (less clear), and no more sufficient (less compelling) than their active voice counterpoints. Moreover, the use of passive voice weakens the sentence's vigor by minimizing the role of the actor while casting the action in a way that often seems limp, listless, and stilted. Note what happens when these famous words are passive-voiced:

Original: Abraham Lincoln, Gettysburg Address, 1863
Now we are engaged in a great civil war, testing whether that nation, or any nation so conceived and so dedicated, can long endure.

Passive Version
A great civil war, testing whether that nation, or any nation so conceived and so dedicated, can long endure is now being engaged in.

Original: John F. Kennedy, Inaugural Address, 1961
My fellow Americans, ask not what your country can do for you, ask what you can do for your country.

Passive Version
My fellow Americans, what your country can do for you should not be asked, what you can do for your country should be asked.

Original: Winston Churchill, First Speech as Prime Minister to House of Commons, 1940
I have nothing to offer but blood, toil, tears, and sweat.

Passive Version
Nothing but blood, toil, tears, and sweat can be offered by me.

Original: Julius Caesar, Report to Roman Senate, 47 B.C.E.
I came, I saw, I conquered.

Passive Version
Coming was accomplished by me, seeing was accomplished by me, conquering was accomplished by me.

Original: The Holy Bible, Old Testament: The Ten Commandments, circa 1500s–1300s B.C.E.
Thou shall not kill.

Passive Version
Killing shall not be done by thou.

Additional examples of passive versus active voice are provided in Box 1.2.

Writers, including many academics, will use passive voice in an attempt to stress the objectivity of their conclusions. *We concluded the following* . . . becomes *The conclusions to be drawn are the following* . . . (Read: *Anybody* would draw the same conclusions we did given the strength of the evidence, which may explain why the sentence has no stated actor.) *The Longman Grammar of Spoken and Written English*, an extensive survey of how writing and speech differ, found that passive voice is used nearly ten times more often in academic writing compared to everyday conversation.[8]

You can give center stage to your findings and still write in active voice by changing the passive sentence's direct object (in this case, *the conclusions*) into the actor. <u>*These conclusions*</u> [actor and subject] *follow from the evidence* . . . Or: *The evidence supports these conclusions* . . .

Seeking to verbally minimize their roles as actors, scholars resort to the kind of passive voice constructions that have come to hallmark academic style. *I will argue* . . . becomes *The argument will be advanced* . . . The better solution, which downplays the imposition of self while still keeping the construction in active voice, makes *paper* the subject of the sentence. *This paper argues* . . . Additional examples:

Passive:	My thesis is supported by scientific evidence.
Active:	Scientific evidence supports my thesis.
Passive:	Both men and women were surveyed by the study.
Active:	The study surveyed both men and women.
Passive:	Several questions were raised by the findings.
Active:	The findings raised several questions.

To write an effective sentence, you must determine what you want your reader to know or do. Framing ideas in active voice generally makes

Box 1.2

Passive	Active
The firm's annual $10,000 award for the best mix of short and long words in a five-page report was won by Max.	Max won the firm's annual $10,000 award for the best mix of short and long words in a five-page report.
A modified payment plan was written by the debtors before they went to jail.	The debtors wrote a modified payment plan before they went to jail.
The decision to strengthen the English Department's Three Strikes Rule on overuse of passive voice was unilaterally made by the dean.	The dean unilaterally decided to strengthen the English Department's Three Strikes Rule on overuse of passive voice.
Our former marketing manager believed that more buying would be engaged in by people during a recession.	Our former marketing manager believed that people would buy more during a recession.
Her pledge never to marry a grammar-challenged man was made by her on her tenth birthday.	On her tenth birthday, she pledged never to marry a grammar-challenged man.
More than two days will be required to write the 200-page report.	The 200-page report will require more than two days to write.
A ten billion dollar accounting error was committed. (missing actor)	The intern committed a ten billion dollar accounting error. (actor added)

it easier for you to see what's happening (or being conditionalized) in the sentence and who is responsible—or *who* (or what) is doing *what* to *whom* (or to *what*). This who-what-whom relationship reflects the dynamic of the typical sentence and must be grasped whenever you write any sentence, even those you strategically put in passive voice.

The use of active voice also enhances your credibility because it portrays you as confident and forthright. You are not afraid to identify and emphasize the actor's role in producing the action. You write, *I mistakenly fired my proofreader*, not *My proofreader was mistakenly fired by me*. Active voice engenders a sensibility where actors take direct responsibility for their actions. Not surprisingly, the best corporate mission statements are written in active voice.

The previous sentence, of course, was written in passive voice, just like this one. All of which raises the question, When is it appropriate to use passive voice?

1. Generally, we emphasize the sentence's action (and who/what was affected) over the sentence's actor when the action is more important than the actor. *All the museum's prized Rembrandt paintings were forged by a master thief.* The significance of the action, the forging of the paintings, is emphasized over the actor, the master thief. *My favorite television program, Writing Styles of the Rich and Famous, was canceled by the network.* Again, the significance of the action, the canceling of the program, is emphasized over the actor, the network.

When the action decidedly overshadows the actor, it is not uncommon to even omit the actor. *All classes were canceled because of the snowstorm* [missing actor: school officials]. *Dogs are not allowed on the beach* [missing actor: city ordinance]. *The CEO was fired* [missing actor: the company's board of directors].

2. Other times, we emphasize the action when the actor is unknown or obvious.

Unknown Actor: *The digital lab was vandalized. My computer was hacked. My flash drive was stolen.* Without knowing the actors in these sentences, you could still write these sentences in active voice—*Someone vandalized the digital lab; Someone hacked my computer; Someone stole my flash drive*—but you would be emphasizing the less important actor over the more significant action.

Obvious Actor: *Josie was elected treasurer of her sorority* [actor: members of Josie's sorority]. *The class assignment will be graded pass/fail* [actor: the teacher]. *My postal mail is always delivered before 10 AM* [actor: the mail carrier].

3. We also emphasize the action when we want to protect the actor by either minimizing or eliminating his/her responsibility.

Minimizing Responsibility: *The crucial files were submitted late by Sarah, so it was decided by Donald we would all work on Christmas Eve to finish the project.*

Eliminating Responsibility: *The crucial files were submitted late, so it was decided we would all work on Christmas Eve to finish the project.*

Although minimizing or eliminating the actor's responsibility is often self-serving, the strategy can function more honorably. The greater good sometimes invites a more diplomatic, team-building approach that obviates individual fault-finding. Similarly, the assigning of personal blame for accidental behavior can be counter-productive. In early child-rearing, for example, some experts contend it is better to focus on the problem and say to the toddler, *The milk was spilled* [passive voice], rather than *You spilled the milk* [active voice].

4. Passive voice can create a closer connection between two related ideas, resulting in a more powerful message. *The candidate made numerous promises. Those promises, however, were never kept.* The passive-voiced second sentence structurally aligns the key element of both sentences, *promises,* to emphasize they were broken. Or, take this example from author William S. Burroughs: *So cheat your landlord if you can and must, but do not try to shortchange the Muse. It cannot be done. You can't fake quality any more than you can fake a good meal.*[9] Here the passive-voiced second sentence effectively underscores and unifies the idea to which all three sentences speak.

5. Passive voice can build suspense or enhance dramatic effect.

● This year's best strategic plan was written by . . . [drum roll] Billy Shakespeare.

● The Citizen of the Year Committee was chaired by none other than a twice-convicted felon.

6. Writers sometimes use passive voice to vary their style. Listing your accomplishments in a job application letter, for example, you might find yourself starting nearly every sentence with yourself as subject. *I did this . . . I did that . . .* Opting for a stylistic change-up that is less *I*-centered, you choose to describe some of your accomplishments in passive voice: *A new company website and Facebook page were also developed* [by me]. Another way to eliminate the repetition of *I* would be to bullet your accomplishments, allowing you to also begin each entry with a skill-describing, action verb that emphasizes what you did.

As the Assistant Manager of the campus bookstore, I accomplished the following:

● Designed a new sales brochure and pin-up calendar

● Supervised a staff of 15

● Trained and mentored nine new employees

● Coordinated all strategic sales campaigns

● Oversaw the budget and approved all allocations

7. Occasionally, the passive-voiced alternative to an active-voiced construction saves words and/or may even read better.

Active: Weak arguments affect the reader's overall perception of whether the writer is credible and to what extent <u>the reader should believe anything the writer says</u>. (25 words)

Passive: Weak arguments affect the reader's overall perception of whether the writer is credible and to what extent <u>anything said should be believed</u>. (22 words)

Which version do *you* like best and why?

As shown, passive-voiced sentences can serve various strategic functions; their use should not be robotically dismissed. However, it is easy to over-employ passive voice and become oblivious to the practice, as you reel off one unnecessary passive sentence after another. Word-processing software with grammar-check features, although not always accurate, can alert you to the problem and help break you of the habit. But only a thorough understanding of passive versus active voice will enable you to assess which construction best serves your purpose.

Renovation Tip

To minimize unnecessary passive voice constructions, try writing your preliminary drafts in first person, liberally using *I* as your sentence's subject. Then, in subsequent drafts, work to eliminate all or most of your *I* references while still keeping your sentences active. For example, instead of saying, *The conclusions to be drawn from the author's work include . . .* , you initially write, *I read the author as concluding . . .* , which then gets changed to *The author concludes . . .* Sentences that lead with *I* usually induce active voice, but not always (e.g., *I was summoned by the court*).

Akin to the unnecessary use of passive voice is the unnecessary use of *nominalization*. Nominalizing is changing a verb, an adjective, or other part of speech into a noun. Like passive verbs, unnecessary nominalization results in wordy constructions that dilute the action expressed. *I investigated the problem* becomes *I undertook an investigation of the problem.* Changing what would otherwise be the sentence's verb (*investigated*) into a noun (*investigation*) leaves the sentence a verb short, requiring the addition of another verb (*undertook*) to grammatically complete the thought. The key action becomes cloaked in a static noun, resulting in a longer sentence that emphasizes the less important action (*undertook*) over the more significant (*investigated*). Similarly, changing an adjective into a noun can result in having to add another, distracting verb to make the sentence work. *The judgment was irresponsible* [adjective] becomes *The judgment was characterized* [added verb] *by irresponsibility* [noun].

Over-nominalizing serves little purpose other than to produce an artificial, ponderous tone, similar to the sound of passive voice, which some seem to think communicates professionalism, sophistication, and intelligence. Personal writing, where the need for such posturing is absent, features minimal nominalization.

Nominalizing, especially the changing of verbs into nouns, can quickly mushroom, the writer transforming every active verb into bloated, stagey phrasing, as seen in these examples:

Verb	Nominalized Form
acquire	seek acquisition
adjust	create an adjustment
alter	make alteration
announce	issue an announcement
conclude	come to a conclusion
decide	arrive at a decision
discuss	engage in a discussion
enroll	activate enrollment
estimate	offer an estimation
evaluate	perform an evaluation
implement	pursue implementation
indicate	give indication
locate	ascertain the location
resume	begin resumption
substitute	make a substitution

Over-nominalization can easily be spotted and corrected. (1) Look for sentences whose main noun expresses an *action* that reflects what is primarily happening in the sentence. These nouns will start with verb forms (for example, *consider*ation) and will frequently have suffixes such as *-sion*, *-tion*, *-ment*, *-ance*, and *-ence*. They will also be closely preceded by an added verb that detours the reader from the sentence's main thought. (2) Delete the added verb and change the nominalized verb into an active verb.

-                de

  They tried to ~~employ~~ persua~~sion on~~ me.

-                           y   e

  Good writers ~~engage in the~~ identif~~ication~~ and eliminat~~ion of~~ unnecessary words.

- She promised to ~~give an~~ endorse~~ment of~~ my book.

-                                   d

  His mastery of grammar ~~produced~~ excite~~ment among~~ the crowd.

- Please ~~commence~~ ship~~ment of~~ the product.

-                        ers

  A lack of funding ~~is a~~ hind~~rance to~~ my research.

- We were afraid to ~~give~~ utter~~ance to~~ any of our views.

-              d

  I ~~made~~ reference ~~to~~ your work.

-                    y

  Speakers ~~make~~ impl~~ications~~; listeners ~~draw~~ infer~~ences~~.

-              ed

  She ~~was~~ appreciat~~ive of~~ his help.

Sometimes the same word represents both its verb and noun forms. In the examples below, *study*, *review*, and *need* serve as nouns before corrective editing turns them into verbs.

- They will ~~conduct a~~ study ~~of~~ the results.
- A senior faculty member will ~~carry out a~~ review ~~of~~ junior faculty.
- We ~~are in~~ need ~~of~~ additional laboratory space.

Related to nominalizing is the unnecessary changing of verbs into adjectives. The result, again, is to unwittingly de-emphasize the main action in the sentence. *She <u>understands</u>* [verb] *the problem* becomes *She <u>is</u>* [added linking verb] *<u>understanding</u>* [predicate adjective] *of the problem. He <u>knows</u>* [verb] *what he is doing* becomes *He <u>is</u>* [added linking verb] *<u>knowledgeable</u>* [predicate adjective] *about what he is doing.* Generally, it is best to describe the action in a sentence with a verb, not an adjective.

Not all nominalizing, however, can, or should, be avoided. Because they typically encompass larger meanings than their verb and adjective counterparts, various nominalizations express certain thoughts better. *Composition* and *communication* (for which there is even a scholarly journal of a similar name—*College Composition and Communication*), for example, signify more than just the actions of *composing* and *communicating*; they summarize what the actions entail and produce. Many other popular nominalizations—such as *conclusion* (verb: conclude), *creation* (verb: create), *destruction* (verb: destroy), *dictatorship* (verb: dictate), *difficulty* (adjective: difficult), *failure* (verb: fail); *honesty* (adjective: honest), *legalization* (adjective: legal); *recommendation* (verb: recommend), and *responsibility* (adjective: responsible), to name but a few—perform a similar function and, as such, take on additional meaning in their noun versus verb/adjective form.

Nominalizations can also economically summarize the action referenced earlier in the sentence or in a preceding sentence.

- The mayor pledged to renovate City Hall, the Contemporary Art Museum, and the Downtown Library, but no <u>renovations</u> ever occurred.

- I petitioned to substitute my blogging experience for English 101, my chatroom background for Public Speaking 101, and an hour-long podcast on sports betting for Statistics 101. For some reason, these <u>substitutions</u> were never approved.

- He argued for this and for that, but none of his <u>arguments</u> swayed the audience. Perhaps he should have taken a course or two in <u>argumentation</u>.

Similar to passive voice, the use of nominalization should be governed by whether it represents the best option for effectively expressing your thought and serving your overall thesis.

Vary Sentence Length

To avoid repetitive, monotonous-sounding sentence patterns that can distract your reader, sentences should vary in length, but they should never be longer or shorter than necessary.

Renovation Tip

One test of readability is to ask, How would I *say* the same thing if my reader were sitting across from me? A club leader will write, *Careful thought and deliberation should take place before we go ahead with any decision that involves the initiation and implementation of a monetary cover charge at club-sponsored socials insofar as the decision might risk the potential accruing of negative publicity and public reaction.* Asked what this means, the club leader replies, *Before we decide to charge everyone to attend our parties, we should consider how people might react to the decision.* If you can orally translate your message into a clearer, more concise message, your original version needs revision.

1. A sentence qualifies as unnecessarily long when it contains more than one main thought or when it becomes so verbally overloaded it confuses the reader. No one wants to spend time maneuvering through the maze of a marathon sentence to discern its meaning.

In *The Elements of Style*, William Strunk and E.B. White observe: "When you become hopelessly mired in a sentence, it is best to start fresh; do not try to fight your way through against the terrible odds of syntax. Usually what is wrong is that the construction has become too involved at some point; the sentence needs to be broken apart and replaced by two or more shorter sentences."[10]

Occasionally, all you need to do is add periods to break the endless sentence.

ORIGINAL   I was told by my friends that Professor Stern, also known as The Writing Czar, subtracted points for every grammar, punctuation, usage, and mechanics mistake, but I didn't think she would deduct so many points from my paper that I would get a terrible score on my first college assignment and end up with the lowest grade in the class, all of which explains why I think I should change direction and not major in English.

REVISION   I was told by my friends that Professor Stern, also known as The Writing Czar, subtracted points for every grammar, punctuation, usage, and mechanics mistake. But I didn't think she would deduct so many points from my paper that I would get a terrible score on my first college assignment and end up with the lowest grade in the class. All of which explains why I think I should change direction and not major in English.

More editing, however, is usually required of long, unreadable sentences.

ORIGINAL   Assuming that Mark and Marla are able to convince the city council, which includes three members who are vegetarians and active in the cause, to commercially rezone the property on which they would like to build their restaurant, The Lion Fillet, and assuming Mark and Marla are also able to persuade potential customers that the eating of exotic game food is healthy, as well as environmentally sound, not to mention all-American, and, finally, assuming that Mark and Marla can guarantee both timely and consistent delivery of game food products from their African and American distributors, their new restaurant should be successful.

In this runaway sentence, the writer's thoughts gallop along unharnessed for 103 words. The sentence's conclusion (*their new restaurant should be successful*) is nearly lost by the time the reader finally reaches the end. Breaking the sentence into shorter ones, with the three main points labeled and parallel-structured, emphasizes the writer's key ideas and ties them more directly to a conclusion that now comes first.

REVISION A   For their new restaurant, The Lion Fillet, to succeed, Mark and Marla must do three things: (1) They must convince the city council, which includes three vegetarian activists, to rezone the proposed restaurant site to commercial property. (2) They must show potential customers that eating exotic game is healthy, environmentally sound, and all-American. (3) They must ensure timely and consistent meat deliveries from their African and American distributors.

Or, instead, the writer could use bullets to highlight the key points of the message.

REVISION B   For their new restaurant, The Lion Fillet, to succeed, Mark and Marla must do three things:

- convince the city council, which includes three vegetarian activists, to rezone the proposed restaurant site to commercial property;
- show potential customers that eating exotic game is healthy, environmentally sound, and all-American; and
- ensure timely and consistent meat deliveries from their African and American distributors.

Long sentences sometimes come about because you opt for a windy preface before getting to the point. The windy preface (in **bold**) wastes time and space by usually stating the obvious.

- **After a thorough and careful review and consideration of the facts** [as if to say you normally do not look closely at the facts?], I determined that Sadie, 72, should not be promoted to Head Bouncer.

Or the windy preface refers to a question or request that could easily be summarized in a subject line at the top of the page, allowing the message to start with what is most important to the reader: your answer.

- **In response to your question about whether we provide free legal services to the rich, the answer is** yes, we provide free legal services to the rich.
- **Per your request,** here is a list of websites that caution against creating your own website.

In the example below, the entire first sentence can be deleted and replaced with a short summary phrase, *policy on delinquent debts*, placed in the subject line. Your message would then lead with the good news.

- **We received your e-mail yesterday inquiring about whether we still break the arms of gamblers who have difficulty paying their debts on time.** We no longer break or sever the limbs of delinquent debtors.

Once you omit the long windup, you may need to add a few words to get the sentence moving.

- **With the desired, planned objective in mind of improving** [To improve] everyone's writing skills, we tied medical benefits to writing proficiencies.
- **As far as our observations are concerned, we found** [We observed] several cases where stronger writers took fewer sick days than weaker writers.

Other slow sentence beginnings, such as starting with *there are*, also weaken the reader's engagement. Deleting the *There are . . . who/that . . .* beginning, which you can do most—not all—of the time, creates a faster, more powerful sentence. ***There are** nine people who want to date me.* In this slow mover, *There are . . . who* adds nothing and intrudes upon the sentence's two key elements: *nine people* and *want to date me.* Besides, it is much more likely that the first words out of anyone facing the delight of this predicament would be *nine people*, not *There are.*

The *There are . . . who/that . . .* construction may come after a dependent clause or a phrase.

- After Sheriff Tuff took over, **there were** fewer cyber-criminals **who** roamed the streets of Computerville.
- In my view, **there are** no rewards **that** justify betraying a rich and generous roommate.

After deleting *There are . . . who/that . . .* , you may find yourself needing to add, change, or rearrange a word or two to make the sentence work.

ORIGINAL	There are few job openings for inexperienced lion tamers.
REVISION	Few job openings exist for inexperienced lion tamers.
ORIGINAL	There is the view held by many murderers that media-portrayed violence is not socially harmful.
REVISION	Many murderers believe that media-portrayed violence is not socially harmful.
ORIGINAL	There are several brilliant ideas about text messaging that I will text to the Conference on Texting.
REVISION	I will text several brilliant ideas about text messaging to the Conference on Texting.

Word choice can also add to a sentence's length. Shorter words (two syllables or less), the runts, allow your writing to be read swiftly; longer words (three syllables or more), the giants, tax and slow the reader. Yet longer words are frequently needed, especially in more formal documents, to express complex, nuanced thought in ways no other, shorter words will quite do. This is notably true in academic writing and, to a lesser extent, certain forms of business writing.

You need not avoid using longer words. But when you use longer words mainly out of habit or just to sound intelligent, you limit the effectiveness of your communication. Always ask yourself: Why am I using the longer word? Do I really need it to express myself? If you cannot justify the longer word semantically, opt for its shorter version. Should you wish to convey a slight change, for example, the better word is *modification* (five syllables) because it is more precise. But to use *modification* when you mean a full-fledged change is both long-winded and misleading. The same can be said when you write *accumulate* (four syllables) instead of *gather* to reference an act that is immediate rather than long term, or when you choose *demonstrate*, not *show*, to describe a simple, non-instructional activity. In these cases, the longer word is space wasting and incorrect. Resorting to longer words than necessary is called, ironically, *sesquipedalianism* (yes, a seven-syllable word).

Once you begin to rethink your use of long words, you will discover that many can be replaced with shorter synonyms without much sacrifice in meaning. You will find that it is just as easy to write, *We need to increase the size of the parking lot*, as it is to say, *The parking lot where we currently domicile personal vehicular transportation must undergo structural augmentation.* You can simply *end* the habit of writing like this or you can choose to *initiate appropriate dismissal action* relative to the habit.

Sometimes you may select the longer word just to vary your style. After writing *aim* and *goal* several times, you might covet an *objective* or two. Just as longer synonyms are sometimes needed to avoid tiresome repetition, a substitute phrase can perform the same task. *But* is concise; *on the other hand*, do you want to say it all the time? And should a long word save you three or four short words, use it.

Your preference, though, should be to pick the shorter word first, when appropriate. Frequently, writers say they use words like *admonishment, endeavor*, and *utilization* in relief of *warning, try*, and *use*. But a look at their writing shows they choose longer words repeatedly before using the shorter versions, if at all. Purists will argue there is no such thing as a synonym because no two words mean exactly the same. Even if you agree, it should not be seen as license to use longer words indiscriminately.

Below is a sample of longer words often overused. Next to each is a shorter, simpler word that can usually serve as a good substitute. Some of the words have more than one meaning, allowing for more than one synonym.

accentuate	highlight	indebtedness	debt
admonition	warning	locality	place
aggregate	total	notification	notice
ameliorate	improve	notwithstanding	despite
appellation	name	numerate	count
component	part	optimum	best
corroborate	confirm	preeminent	top
effectuate	effect	prognosticate	predict
elucidate	clarify	remunerate	pay
endeavor	try	salutation	greeting
erroneous	wrong	substantiate	prove
expenditure	expense	trepidation	fear
illumination	light	utilize	use

Another cause of unnecessarily long sentences is verbal inflation. Sometimes, writers strategically want to inflate the facts (note, for instance, the onslaught of modifying adjectives and adverbs in self-written personality profiles appearing in social media). Other times, writers simply fall back on weak, scrawny words whose meaning requires bolstering by adjectives and adverbs.

When adjectives and adverbs, in turn, are insufficient and need their own additional modification, the problem escalates. Many modifying words, such as *very*, function as little more than the writer's concession of having chosen anemic language, a problem *very* will not remedy. Mark Twain is often credited with having said, "Substitute 'damn' every time you're inclined to write 'very'; your editor will delete it and the writing will be just as it should be."

Richard Weaver, in *The Ethics of Rhetoric*, argues that the excessive use of adjectives and adverbs signifies a lesser writer.

> The adjective is . . . a word of secondary status and force. Its burden is an attribute, or something added. In the order of being to which reference has been made, the noun can exist without the adjective, but not the adjective without the noun. . . . The adjective is question-begging; that is to say, if the thing to be expressed is real, it will be expressed through a substantive [a word or group of words that function as a noun]; if it is expressed mainly through adjectives, there is something defective in its reality, since it has gone for secondary support. [The same, he says, holds true for the adverb.][11]

Weaver concedes there are "situations in which such modifiers do make a useful contribution, but as a general rule . . . a style is stronger when it depends mainly upon substantives sharp enough to convey their own attributes."[12]

Personal writing features minimal modification because it is usually unneeded. Writer and reader share the kind of relationship that allows the writer to include less detail and qualification because they will either be filled in by the reader or seen as contextually unimportant. Additionally, the character limits of Twitter, as well as the physical constraints of tweeting (and texting) on smaller keyboards, discourage expending any more key strokes than absolutely necessary. What emerges is a verb-oriented, active-voice style where writers shy away from all but the most essential adjectives and adverbs.

Whereas personal writing rewards easy-to-read sentences that get to the point quickly and efficiently, formal writing is more reliant on modifying language to ensure its sufficiency because the standards of evaluation are far more rigorous. Used judiciously and effectively, modification allows you to express ideas with greater precision, detail, and qualification. But the ease with which modifying words and phrases can enter your text, as if they had a will of their own, should alert you to continually question: Is the modification absolutely needed or can it be deleted without diminishing the text? And if modification is needed, have I made the best choice?

2. A sentence qualifies as shorter than necessary when it abridges the essence of what you want to convey. Because the short sentence is often championed with cult-like admiration, some writers want to break every long sentence, however competently written. This burdens the reader with the task of having to connect two or more parts of a logical whole. An otherwise acceptable sentence should not be severed into multiple sentences unless you intend to express multiple thoughts. The problem of sentence slicing taken to the extreme can be seen in this example:

ORIGINAL My dog has three legs. She weighs 150 pounds. She is blind in one eye. She is missing both her ears. She runs a quarter mile in under a minute.

REVISION Although my dog has three legs, weighs 150 pounds, suffers blindness in one eye, and is missing both her ears, she still manages to run a quarter mile in under a minute.

Which version best communicates the *single* thought that your challenged dog is one fast (and fat) Chihuahua? And lest we forget the big dogs, which of these versions more efficiently connects the conclusion with the supporting rationale?

ORIGINAL Great Danes are smart. They are affectionate. They are loyal. For these reasons I love the big fellas.

REVISION I love Great Danes because they are smart, affectionate, and loyal.

In the revision, four short sentences (18 words total) are combined into one (still short) sentence of 11 words that better communicates the writer's thought. The rewrite also avoids the choppy, childlike-sounding effect that can occur when short sentences are strung together.

A well-crafted, well-positioned short sentence can adeptly communicate your point. *The candidate for student body president actually claimed he could reduce tuition, increase parking, lower the cost of textbooks, and create a winning football program. Then again, it is election season.* But thinking and composing exclusively or even ostensibly in short sentences can easily foster a preoccupation with reportage as opposed to analysis and synthesis. Insofar as language and thought are inseparable (our thinking influences our language choices; our language choices influence our thinking), an over-reliance on short sentences may unwittingly lead writer and reader to adopt a breezy, surface view of the world that fails to consider how various elements relate to, and affect, one another.

In general, you need longer sentences to express more complex and nuanced thought. Academic writing, in particular, often mandates the type of detailed explanation and qualification that increases sentence length. The long sentence should not be avoided if it conveys what the short sentence cannot. Nevertheless, a style laden with long sentences, no matter how concise and elegant, challenges the reader's processing skills, while one that relies only on short sentences can reflect simplistic thought. An appropriate mixture of short and long sentences provides the best of both worlds.

Eliminate Unnecessary and Unneeded Words

It is easier to see what a sentence is saying, what it needs to say, and where it fits in the paragraph—or if it fits at all—when you streamline its content and expose its core. Revising clunky passages by trimming unnecessary words reveals the essence of your thought. Stripped of distracting verbiage, a sentence's meaning and purpose become more transparent.

Although we speak of them in the same breath, clarity and conciseness are not always complementary. Usually, the more concisely you write, the clearer your message. But if you exclude vital information to achieve conciseness, your clarity will suffer—as will your conciseness if you keep restating content for the sake of clarity.

Conciseness is not a matter of just writing shorter sentences. A sentence of 30, 40, or even 50 words is concise if its main thought cannot be effectively conveyed in fewer words. And a sentence of ten words is inconcise if it can be said as well in six or seven words. Conciseness means using the fewest words necessary, regardless of the number, to express yourself as cogently as possible without compromising the whole of your thought. The aim is to craft messages that are simple, not simplistic, by cutting the fat not the muscle. Every word must pull its weight.

Nor is conciseness a matter of just eliminating supporting facts/statistics, examples, or testimony. Indeed, it is not unusual for a message to be both wordy and incomplete: the writer presents a verbose conclusion—*I am of the considerable opinion that it would prove to be beneficial for all concerned parties if we were to achieve a reduction in student enrollment in all the remedial courses we teach*—and then fails to support the conclusion with sufficient evidence and reasoning. Conciseness does not equal the absence of proof. An incomplete message is hardly compelling.

The first step in purging any message of its wordiness is *not* to look for entire paragraphs or pages to cut, but to make sure every word is needed. Even a relatively short message can be twice as long as necessary.

ORIGINAL

This is to inform you that we have your order dated March 16 for four dozen gold Spy Pens with disappearing ink, for which we want to express our thanks.

We regret to advise you that we are no longer making this pen in gold and hereby wish to advise that we are currently producing it only in black. However, we do have a gold-colored Advanced Spy Pen with disappearing ink, which includes a self-destruction switch. The Advanced Spy Pen with disappearing ink and self-destruction switch costs an extra $9.95 per unit. Please indicate whether you wish us to ship you four dozen black Spy Pens with disappearing ink or four dozen gold Advanced Spy Pens with disappearing ink and self-destruction switch.

We shall be awaiting your kind response on this matter.

REVISION

Thank you for your March 16 order for four dozen gold Spy Pens with disappearing ink.

We now make this pen in black only. However, our Advanced Spy Pen with disappearing ink and self-destruction switch is available in gold, but it costs an extra $9.95 per pen. Would you like us to fill your order with black Spy Pens or gold Advanced Spy Pens?

In the revision, 64 words do the work of the 132 in the original. The writer gets to the point more efficiently, and the closing question, unlike the original's weak ending, invites action. Eliminating wordiness increases the chance your audience will read, understand, and act on your message.

Pleonasm, the use of more words than necessary, afflicts much of today's writing. Pleonastic examples are so common we seldom stop to consider what they really mean. When we do, we realize how little they say. Note the variations of this familiar opening:

We'd like to talk with you . . .

> on the matter of
> in connection with
> in reference to
> in relation to
> on the subject of
> with regard to
> with respect to . . . our new cell phones.

One word, *about*, could replace any of the above prepositional phrases, leading to a tighter sentence.

"Clutter," says William Zinsser, in *On Writing Well*, "is the disease of American writing. We are a society strangling in unnecessary words, circular constructions, pompous frills and meaningless jargon."[13] Such writing comes about in part because we want to sound intelligent and professional. Self-conscious about how we project, we embrace an artificial, lofty-aspiring style where needless complexity rules the page. We equate pretentious tone with sophistication, unnatural formality with elegance, meandering sentences with profoundness. Focusing more on ourselves than on our readers, we produce the sort of wordy, affected writing we would never dream of speaking. Descartes said, *I think, therefore I am.*[14] The word hoarder says, *I engage in cognitive processing that functions ultimately to substantiate my real-world existence.* Shakespeare said, *Cowards die many* times before their deaths; *The valiant never taste of death but once.*[15] The word hoarder says, *Those having a character that reflects timidity will metaphorically experience extinction often, but those having a character that reflects courage will literally experience extinction once.*

Most of the stilted wordiness plaguing poor writing is learned. The text swelling starts as soon as you get that first of many school writing assignments having a minimum word requirement: "Papers must be at least 1500 words." You begin, *This essay describes the political system of the United Kingdom.* Then you count: 10 words; 1490 to go. I'm never going to finish. Okay, let me try stretching it a bit. *This essay has chosen a very important subject area that is worthy of study, which is consequently the reason why it was selected as the topic for this term paper. The country that is known as the United Kingdom will be discussed in terms of its political system in the subsequent pages that will be presented.* You count again: 56 words. Now that's more like it; only 1444 to go!

Later, when you enter the workforce, you learn to become even wordier, this time spurred by the corporate sense of what sounds business-like. *We received your complaint today and will investigate the matter* is edited by your first supervisor to read, *Your complaint has been officially received and recorded, as of today, and it will be investigated further by our staff in an appropriate manner.* Meanwhile, down the hallway in another meeting, upper management is complaining about the problems of poor employee writing.

Renovation Tip

Minimum word requirements discourage conciseness because they reward you for adding more text. Instead, imagine having to stay within a *maximum* word limit. Take any writing assignment that does not have a strict minimum word or page requirement. Estimate how long your paper is likely to run based upon your having completed similar assignments. Now cut the estimate by one-third and use this figure as your strict maximum. Forced to write concisely, you will.

The easiest editing is when you can delete extra words without having to add or change other words in the sentence.

- **In order** to **totally** finish **the completion of** my book on the history of the question mark, I wrote **all** throughout **the months of** July and August.
- We should eliminate **the occurrence of** wordiness **as of** now, not by **the** early **part of** next month.
- The **issue in** question is whether **or not** he would have been elected Homecoming King prior to **the start of** his learning to write well.
- **It is** often **the case that** good writers are also good lovers.
- **A woman named** Linda, who has a Ph.D. in **the field of** English, told me so.

A single word can frequently replace several others without changing the sentence's meaning.

- We hold conciseness seminars **on a monthly basis** [monthly], but we would like to hold them **on a weekly basis** [weekly].
- This **is a** check **in the amount of** [for] $50 **to** cover[s] the bet I lost on apostrophes.

  Or

  This $50 check covers the bet I lost on apostrophes.
- We could not complete the report on time **due to the fact that** [because] our editor was arrested for stealing composition books.
- Your argument **is based on the assumption** [assumes] the famous self-help author lied about having 47 assistants.
- Iris eyed the report **for the purpose of** [to] **examining** [examine] the facts.
- **In light of the fact that** [Because] he does not know how to write a complete sentence, he should be fired.

  Or

  He should be fired because he does not know how to write a complete sentence.

Or

He does not know how to write a complete sentence and should be fired.

● She performed best **in any situation in which** [when] she was asked to revise quickly.

● My editorial responsibilities were always **in a state of change** [changing] **in the course of** [during] my career at Evolving Industries.

● **During the time of my stay** [while] at MIT, I studied the writing habits of wrestling coaches **all over the world** [worldwide].

You could also say *At MIT*, but the meaning would be slightly different. *While at MIT* suggests you went to MIT mainly to study something other than the writing habits of wrestling coaches. *At MIT* implies you went to MIT primarily to study their writing habits.

● I **am of the thought that** [think] your **use of** syntax is breathtaking.

That can usually be deleted if its absence does not create an awkward or confusing sentence. Note, however, the initial reader misdirection that occurs when *that* is eliminated in these sentences: *I told Buddy the bear* [a friend of Smokey Bear?] *was eating our writing journals.* (**Revision**: *I told Buddy that the bear . . .*) *It was the lion Buddy* [another animal named Buddy?] *was trying to avoid.* (**Revision**: *It was the lion that Buddy . . .*) *I believe the lion* [because the lion has credibility?] *was friendlier before we named him.* (**Revision**: *I believe that the lion . . .*)

● **Any number of** [many, some] novelists believe their books will be bestsellers.

In this example, the sentence is both wordy and inconcise. How many is *any number of?*

Sometimes a simple change in punctuation allows you to delete words and collapse two or more sentences into one that's shorter and better.

ORIGINAL   I have five favorite punctuation marks. They are commas, semicolons, colons, dashes, and ellipses.

REVISION   I have five favorite punctuation marks: commas, semicolons, colons, dashes, and ellipses.

ORIGINAL   My treatise on semicolons will appeal to two groups. One group would be people who love punctuation. The other group would be people with a lot of time on their hands.

REVISION   My treatise on semicolons will appeal to two groups: people who love punctuation, and people with a lot of time on their hands.

ORIGINAL   I love to read novels. Another one of my loves is poetry, and I also love literary nonfiction.

REVISION   I love to read novels, poetry, and literary nonfiction.

ORIGINAL   My footnoting skills include familiarity with all major style guides. I learned these skills when I was on academic probation.

REVISION   My footnoting skills, learned when I was on academic probation, include familiarity with all major style guides.

The preceding sampling of wordy sentences illustrates how even the shortest of content can be inconcise. Lengthier sentences, a staple of academic writing, can usually be streamlined even more.

ORIGINAL   Although there are numerous cases of the writer's lack of critical thinking skills that abound, the purpose of this paper is to focus on three of those specific examples in question, each one very much representing a different aspect of the problem. (42 words)

REVISION   Although numerous cases of the writer's lack of critical thinking skills abound, this paper focuses on three examples, each representing a different aspect of the problem. (26 words)

ORIGINAL   The accuracy and veracity of the journalist's personality pieces were rarely ever challenged by the individuals the journalist depicted, primarily because many of the people with whom the journalist had interacted and subsequently depicted had no interest in providing corrective response, or they were not in a position to have the means to provide corrective response to the journalist's writings. (60 words)

REVISION   The accuracy of the journalist's personality pieces was rarely challenged by the individuals depicted, many of whom had neither the interest nor the means to provide corrective response. (28 words)

ORIGINAL   Satirical oxymorons have as their function the expression of political and social viewpoints through the referring of their targeted subject, the one meant to be satirized, as "oxymoronic"—for example, *military intelligence, civil engineer, Microsoft Works*—or by the coupling of their targeted subject with a word that is usually viewed to be a positive descriptor, with the writer then referring back to the construction created as "oxymoronic," as seen in such examples as *honest* politician, *compassionate* IRS agent, or *smart* reality show star. (84 words)

REVISION   Satirical oxymorons express political and social viewpoints by referring to their targeted subject as "oxymoronic"—for example, *military intelligence, civil engineer, Microsoft Works*—or by coupling their targeted subject with a positive descriptor and then labeling the term "oxymoronic," as in *honest* politician, *compassionate* IRS agent, or *smart* reality show star. (51 words)

Once your consciousness is raised and you become sensitized to the siren of verbal excess and the many ways that "habit phrases" fatten your writing, you can quickly detect and revise them.

Below are more examples of phrases that squander your reader's time. Next to each is one word, sometimes two, having nearly the same meaning.

a large number of	many, most
all of a sudden	suddenly
as a matter of fact	in fact
as of late	lately
at a future date	later
at the present time	now

at this juncture	now
enclosed herewith	enclosed
despite the fact that	although
has the implication	implies
in a timely manner	timely
in order that	so
in recognition of this fact	hence, thus
in the event that	if
is able to	can
is an example of	exemplifies
is an illustration of	illustrates
is responsible for choosing	chooses
it is apparent that	apparently
it would seem that	seemingly
make it possible	enable
make provisions for	provide
negate the possibility of	preclude
notwithstanding the fact that	although, despite
on a continual basis	continually
on the decrease	decreasing
on the grounds that	because
read through	read
somewhere in the neighborhood of	around
the ability to	can
we are of the opinion	we think

Occasionally, the wordier version is preferable to its shorter counter-part. It is more concise to say *disabled person* than *person with a disability*, but the primary positioning of *disabled* in *disabled person* highlights the disability and serves to define the person. *Person with a disability* is wordier, but it emphasizes the person over the disability, which is demoted to a secondary role. At other times, you may want to emphasize a point, say, a key statistic, by later reiterating it, using somewhat different, perhaps slightly longer, wording. For example, rather than repeating verbatim, *Forty-eight percent of Americans believe* . . . , you write, *As noted, nearly one-half of all Americans believe* . . . , or *Remember, nearly one in two Americans believes* . . . Here the longer version of the same idea allows you to avoid stylistic repetition and drive home your point in yet another way.

Most wordiness can be eliminated by closely editing your text line by line. Sometimes, though, only a new draft will do. If you find yourself reading a passage much longer than necessary and not knowing where to begin editing, it may be best to start from scratch.

ORIGINAL   I am eager to solicit any and all editing suggestions that you may wish to make, and you can be assured that each and every such recommendation will be given my utmost, careful review. (34 words)

REVISION   I welcome your editing suggestions, which I will review carefully. (10 words)

ORIGINAL   We wish to advise you that we have thoroughly and completely examined your July travel expense transactions request form, and we have decided to make an affirmative recommendation regarding your request for reimbursement. Your claim for $9 travel reimbursement has been granted. (42 words)

REVISION   We approved your $9 travel reimbursement request. (7 words)

ORIGINAL   If we continue to defer maintenance operations through our failure to supply sufficient funds to make needed repairs as they naturally become necessary from time to time, the operating efficiency of the Mash Pit Arena will steadily diminish to the point that the situation will be able to be corrected only by our undertaking of a major construction project. (59 words)

REVISION   If we continually fail to repair the Mash Pit Arena when the need arises, the problems will worsen and eventually cost more to fix. (24 words)

Renovation Tip

When you mercilessly delete unneeded words, your revised sentences may start to sound choppy.

- She believed she was the company's most productive employee. She trained and mentored scores of other employees over the years. She asked for a promotion and a raise. The company refused her request. She quit. She started her own business a month later.

Adding words that signal and bridge your thoughts can help you transition between thoughts more smoothly.

- She believed she was the company's most productive employee. *Additionally*, she trained and mentored scores of other employees over the years. *So*, she asked for a promotion and a raise. *Thus*, when the company refused her request, she quit. She *subsequently* started her own business a month later.

As your writing improves and your structure and style become more fluid, your sentences will follow one another more naturally, creating less need for these connectors.

- She believed she was the company's most productive employee. She even trained and mentored scores of employees over the years. But when the company refused her request for a raise and promotion, she quit. A month later, she started her own business.

What about contractions in terms of saving words? In informal writing, contractions create a natural, conversational tone. And they consume less space by turning two words into one. Uncontracted forms, however, can underscore certain ideas more effectively. Greater warning, for example, is conveyed by *You should not* than *You shouldn't*. The longer form, *not*, also allows for additional formatting emphasis, such as *not*, **not**, NOT, or NOT (small capitals). Similarly, *We will decide* is stronger than *We'll decide*.

When convention calls for a more elevated style, such as in most formal documents, the use of contractions, abbreviations (including text message abbreviations), colloquialisms, and exclamation marks will seem out of place. In *Fumblerules: A Lighthearted Guide to Grammar and Good Usage*, William Safire expresses the orthodoxy: "You don't wear a tie to a ballgame, and you do not wear loafers to a church wedding. In the same way, you shouldn't use formal English when your intent is to be sassy and breezy, nor should you employ contractions in a solemn speech or formal letter."[16]

An unanticipated advantage of using contractions is their spawning of a mindset that induces more readable writing. Edward P. Bailey, Jr. notes in *The Plain English Approach to Business Writing* that employing contractions improves your "write-ability" because they lead to shorter, simpler, more direct sentence constructions. The same writer who would ordinarily say, *Don't do it*, will unconsciously adopt the stiffer, longer style the un-contracted form seems to engender: *Do not participate in such activities at this time.* Bailey suggests writing everything first with contractions to ensure readability, after which formal documents can be "*un*contracted."[17]

Renovation Tip

Because grade schoolers tend to start so many of their written and spoken sentences with *and* and *but*, teachers, out of frustration, often come to proclaim, emphatically and unequivocally, that sentences should **never** begin with such conjunctions. But, in fact, no grammatical rule forbids it. And, of course, nothing precludes you from beginning a sentence with any coordinating conjunction (*and, but, or, nor, for, so, yet*). As experienced writers know, the occasional, strategic breaking of an otherwise single sentence into two, with the second sentence starting with *and* or *but*, emphasizes the second sentence, which can be especially effective when it contrasts with the first.

- He claimed to have studied ten hours a day, seven days a week, fifty-two weeks a year. And yet, he never received a grade higher than B–.

- She took Biology 101, 102, 103, 202, 203, 204, 205, 306, 307, 308, 309, 409, 410, 411, 412, and 413. But she was never a Biology major.

Many people have also been taught never to start a sentence with *because*. A subordinating conjunction, *because* introduces a dependent clause, meaning that when a sentence begins with *because* it must be completed by an independent clause. *Because it's okay to begin a sentence with a conjunction* is not a complete sentence; it is a dependent clause. *Because it's okay to begin a sentence with a conjunction, I decided to do so from time to time,* however, is a complete sentence because the introductory dependent clause precedes an independent clause. A sentence can begin with *because* as long as what follows is a complete sentence.

Starting a sentence with *because* makes good sense when you want to emphasize the dependent clause. Note how the first example, compared to the second, highlights Betty's feat.

- Because she wrote so spectacularly, Betty tutored college composition students while she was still in high school.
- Betty tutored college composition students while she was still in high school because she wrote so spectacularly.

Too, some advise against starting a sentence with *too* or *however.* However well-meaning this counsel, it is neither rules-based nor otherwise warranted.

EXERCISES

Exercise 1

Identify the incomplete sentences and then rewrite them as complete sentences.

A. Unable to complete the assignment because I got sick the day it was due.

B. Even though my roommate studies more than I did and always received better grades than I did.

C. Once I meet the requirements the department has established for enrolling in an internship, which won't be easy because several courses are listed as prerequisites and must be taken in sequence.

D. Publish or perish!

E. They concluded.

F. Despite my efforts to learn the differences between a complete and incomplete sentence.

G. If I am right.

H. After the teacher gave back our papers and explained how we could all improve our grades by simply following directions.

I. He snores.

J. Because you won't be attending class today.

Exercise 2

De-bloat this sentence.

> In our endeavor to determine whether the proposal we have formulated for a nudist colony in downtown Santa Barbara is fundamentally sound, we anticipate engaging the services of a market research organization to ascertain whether our conceptualization of the market can be substantiated by information accumulated by empirical, scientific research.

Exercise 3

Change this paragraph, now in passive voice, into active voice.

The A+ on my last paper was deserved. My arguments were developed and structured flawlessly; they were also sequenced beautifully. And my paper was punctuated perfectly. Most of all, my personality—thoughtful, organized, detailed, and modest—was captured by my essay.

Exercise 4

Change this paragraph, now in active voice, into passive voice.

At first, I thought my professor did not like me because she insisted I needed to improve my writing skills. She suggested several ways how I could get better. I followed all her advice. I improved my writing skills, and several employers took me more seriously. Although most of my friends received one or two job offers after graduation, five companies offered me a job. Because of my strong writing skills, my current employer just promoted me again. Now I think my professor did like me.

Exercise 5

Change the nominalized verb in each of these sentences back to an active verb and revise the sentence.

A. You must make payment of your parking fines.

B. We should provide distribution of our new academic dishonesty policy to all students.

C. State officials announced they will administer an audit of all for-profit colleges and universities.

D. Darla is a consistent winner of our Writer of the Month award.

E. Students who know how to fix unnecessary nominalizations should render assistance to those who don't.

Exercise 6

Enhance the readability of this sentence, a 79-word monstrosity, by breaking it into two or more clear, concise, and compelling sentences. Be sure your rewrite includes all the key points in the original sentence.

In accordance with the director's recent authorization to formalize arrangements with Dr. Renovation, who will be conducting a series of workshops for us with the purpose of simplifying, clarifying, and making more readable those written materials integral to the effective functioning of the company, the director requests that samples of all written materials, typical of those prepared by each manager, be forwarded to the director by Monday in order that they can be given to Dr. Renovation for commentary.

Exercise 7

Fast start these slow starts by cutting and/or revising the offending material.

A. I will now present my objections to your proposal, which come in the form of five reasons.

B. In addressing your concerns about why I have been late to class eight times, I would like to say that I have never come to class late intentionally.

C. You have asked me to give you my responses to the ten questions you have posed of me, which I will now do.

D. There are no social dating websites devoted to matching Christians, Jews, and Muslims who share a mutual interest in writing clearly, concisely, and compellingly.

E. There are some sentences that may need to start with *there are*, but this is not one of them.

Exercise 8

Replace each word with at least one shorter synonym of two syllables or less.

additional _____

altercation _____

anticipate _____

approximately _____

assistance _____

commitment _____

compensate _____

culminate _____

encounter _____

equivalent _____

fundamental _____

maintenance _____

necessitate _____

proficiency _____

recollection _____

subsequent _____

terminate _____

Exercise 9

Revise each wordy phrase down to one word.

at an early date _____

for the reason that _____

has the ability to _____

in large measure _____

in the near future _____

in the vicinity of _____

is a representation of   _____

is an indication of   _____

is based on the inference   _____

it is evident that   _____

it is probable that   _____

most of the time   _____

offers the suggestion   _____

on a regular basis   _____

on the increase   _____

performs the function of   _____

take the place of   _____

to a large degree   _____

Exercise 10

Revise this paragraph, making it more clear, concise, and compelling.

> The various activities of the technical personnel of the Research and Development Department have the common objective of acquiring knowledge and making profitable application of this knowledge within the company's sphere of operations. The mechanics of successfully achieving this objective include the inception of ideas; their experimental trial; the evaluation of experimental results; and, where economically attractive, the adaptation of resultant developments to practice.

Exercise 11

Your mission, should you choose to accept: restore these famous statements from the worlds of film and television back to their original eloquence.

A. I am unequivocally directing you to immediately demonstrate your capacity to monetarily enrich me.

B. I will extend a proposal to the individual in question, the terms of which are of such an attractive nature that the chances of his rendering a rejection of the offer are not likely.

C. I guarantee with utmost certainty my revisitation of body and mind upon the situation in which we currently find ourselves.

D. Are you offering what should be viewed as your preliminary response regarding your position on the question, or are you presenting a more definitive conclusion that represents the finality of your thinking?

E. Apparently, you are under the impression that you can engage in terpsichorean activity with success.

Exercise 12

Write a complete short story, with a beginning, a middle, and an end, using a maximum of 55 words. Your story must have a setting, one or more characters (you could be one of the characters), and some kind of conflict that gets resolved at the end. For a discussion of the nature and structure of 55-word short stories and how their authorship promotes cogent writing, see Chapter 6.

Notes

1   McNamara, Mary. "'Night' Moves." Review of *The Night Of*, HBO. *Los Angeles Times*, July 9, 2016, p. E5.

2   Fish, Stanley. *How to Write a Sentence and How to Read One*. Harper, 2011, p. 37.

3   See Barzun, Jacques. *Simple & Direct: A Rhetoric for Writers*. Harper & Row, 1975.

4   Wolfe, Tom. Quoted in symposium, "The New Journalism." *Writer's Digest*, Jan. 1970, p. 19.

5   Plath, Sylvia. *The Unabridged Journals of Sylvia Plath*. Edited by Karen V. Kukil, Anchor, 2000, p. 43.

6   Capote, Truman. *In Cold Blood: A True Account of a Multiple Murder and Its Consequences*. Random House, 1965, p. 5.

7   Eco, Umberto. *The Island of the Day Before*. Houghton Mifflin Harcourt, 2006, p. 366.

8   Biber, Douglas, et al. *Longman Grammar of Spoken and Written English*. Pearson, 1999, pp. 476–80, 937–40.

9   Burroughs, William S. *The Western Lands*. Viking, 1987, p. 4.

10   Strunk, William, and E. B.White. *The Elements of Style*. Macmillan, 1959, p. 65.

11   Weaver, Richard. *The Ethics of Rhetoric*, Henry Regnery, 1953, p. 129.

12   Weaver, p. 129.

13   Zinsser, William. *On Writing Well*. Harper & Row, 1976, p. 6.

14   Descartes, René. *Discourse on the Method of Rightly Conducting One's Reason and of Seeking Truth in the Sciences*, 1637 (quotation found in part IV).

15   Shakespeare, William. *The Tragedy of Julius Caesar*, 1599 (quotation found in Act II, Scene II).

16   Safire, William. *Fumblerules: A Lighthearted Guide to Grammar and Good Usage*. Dell, 1990, p. 14.

17   Bailey, Edward P. Jr. *The Plain English Approach to Business Writing*. Oxford University Press, 1990, pp. 21–22.

Constructing Paragraphs and Pages

2

Moving from Sentences to Paragraphs

Rally around the Topic Sentence

A paragraph is a unit of composition that supports your thesis statement. Generally, a paragraph (excluding your paragraphs of introduction and conclusion) establishes one main idea/main argument summarized by a *topic sentence*, typically the paragraph's first sentence, and developed, directly or indirectly, by the rest of the paragraph. The topic sentence is your promise of what your readers will find in the paragraph. When you do not follow through with this pledge—when your paragraph does not develop its topic sentence or when it includes material not on point—your readers are led astray. Usually, your topic sentence is declarative. (For an example of when it might not be, see Exercise 2.)

Not every paragraph must begin with a topic sentence. When a long paragraph is broken into two or more paragraphs to make it easier to read, the second and subsequent paragraphs can continue to develop the topic sentence introduced in the first paragraph. You do not need to formally reintroduce your topic sentence, although you may want to remind your reader of the paragraph's purpose as you start your new paragraphs. *Another example of why . . .*

It is customary not to have topic sentences in narrative writing, where they would halt the flow of the story. Narrative style is central to journalism and fiction; it appears less in academic and business writing, which feature more overt structuring and labeling of main ideas/main arguments.

A descriptive paragraph may not require a topic sentence if its purpose is apparent. If you were to describe a friend's physical features, for example, you would likely start with one feature and then move to the next. Your reader would almost immediately know what you were doing. You would not need the topic sentence, *I will describe the physical features of my friend*. In persuasive messages, the absence of topic sentences is unusual, although you may occasionally conclude that your argument is so evident throughout the paragraph that a topic sentence would come across as clumsy overkill.

Another reason for not employing a topic sentence is when you decide that the paragraph's main idea/main argument will have more impact if the reader, not the writer, completes it. Executing this strategy, however, requires first-rate writing skills. You must be capable of holding the attention of your reader—who is given no immediate sense of where the paragraph is going—while you nimbly steer toward the paragraph's main idea/main argument.

You may choose to place a topic sentence somewhere other than at the top of the paragraph. Should you perceive your paragraph's main idea/main argument to be so off-putting to readers that it stands a better chance of acceptance if it comes after you have first presented its supporting evidence, you can adopt a climactic approach (further discussed later in the chapter), where you end the paragraph with your topic sentence. More often, however, it is the writer's tone, not the decision to start with a controversial idea/argument, that alienates audiences.

Sometimes, writers delay introducing a topic sentence because they want to "set the stage" for what follows. They lead with a transitional state-ment in the form of an internal summary, followed by the topic sentence.

> If you believe that a losing record and the degrading treatment of players are not enough to justify firing the coach, think again. The most pressing reason is that he is a racist.

Frequently, these paragraph-opening transitions and internal summaries can be combined into the topic sentence. *Besides his losing record and degrading treatment of players, the coach should be fired because he is a racist.* Still, time and again, writers waste paragraph beginnings on unnecessary prologue before getting to the topic sentence. *Now I will discuss the issue of racism. The coach is racist.*

A good topic sentence makes the paragraph not only easier to read and remember, but easier to write. Think of it as a mantra that guides your efforts and keeps you focused. Even when it stays in your head and never makes the page, the topic sentence controls everything you do in the paragraph. Or, to use another metaphor: it is the foundation on which you attach and build your thoughts. Whether you explicitly state your topic sentence or whether it implicitly resides in your text, it directs what you say and how you say it.

Stay Unified

When you first compose your topic sentence, consider it a "working," or tentative, version that you may need to revise once you complete the paragraph and can view all your sentences at once. Asking these questions can help you evaluate the effectiveness of your topic sentence: Does every sentence in the paragraph either directly support the topic sentence or shore up other sentences that support the topic sentence? If not, should I revise my topic sentence to encompass all the sentences that follow, or would it be better to edit, add, or delete sentences to bring the supporting text in line with my topic sentence? Or must I fix both my topic sentence and one or more supporting sentences to ensure a unified paragraph, where every sentence comes together in common cause to support my topic sentence?

One way of identifying which sentences do not belong in the paragraph is by determining whether each sentence answers the same basic question the topic sentence would if it were turned into a question. For example, *The coach is racist* answers the question, Is the coach racist? All sentences in the paragraph, to be unified, must address this question in some way. When they do not, they should be revised, deleted, or moved elsewhere in the message under topic sentences they do support.

What most writers find tougher to delete are eloquent sentences not on point. They become so enamored with their own words they hesitate to part with any of them. A sentence, no matter how impressive in thought and execution, must still speak to the message at hand. In *Style: Toward Clarity and Grace*, Joseph M. Williams observes:

> There is more to readable writing than local clarity. A series of clear sentences can still be confusing if we fail to design them to fit their context, to reflect a consistent point of view, to emphasize our most important ideas.[1]

Box 2.1 embellishes Lincoln's Gettysburg Address to include famous portions of other speeches. Which five sentences do not belong?

Box 2.1

Four score and seven years ago our fathers brought forth on this continent, a new nation, conceived in Liberty, and dedicated to the proposition that all men are created equal. Let every nation know, whether it wishes us well or ill, that we shall pay any price, bear any burden, meet any hardship, support any friend, oppose any foe, to assure the survival and the success of liberty.

Now we are engaged in a great civil war, testing whether that nation, or any nation so conceived and so dedicated, can long endure. We are met on a great battlefield of that war. We have come to dedicate a portion of that field, as a final resting place for those who here gave their lives that that nation might live. It is altogether fitting and proper that we should do this. The future doesn't belong to the fainthearted; it belongs to the brave.

But, in a larger sense, we cannot dedicate—we cannot con-secrate—we cannot hallow—this ground. I have nothing to offer but blood, toil, tears, and sweat. The brave men, living and dead, who struggled here, have consecrated it, far above our poor power to add or detract. The world will little note, nor long remember what we say here, but it can never forget what they did here. We hold these truths to be self-evident, that all men are created equal, that they are endowed by their Creator with certain unalienable rights, that among these are life, liberty and the pursuit of happiness. It is for us the living, rather, to be dedicated here to the unfinished work which they who fought here have thus far so nobly advanced. It is rather for us to be here dedicated to the great task remaining before us—that from these honored dead we take increased devotion to that cause for which they gave the last full measure of devotion—that we here highly resolve that these dead shall not have died in vain—that this nation, under God, shall have a new birth of freedom—and that government of the people, by the people, for the people, shall not perish from the earth. The only thing we have to fear is fear itself.

Box 2.2

Four score and seven years ago our fathers brought forth on this continent, a new nation, conceived in Liberty, and dedicated to the proposition that all men are created equal. [1] *Let every nation know, whether it wishes us well or ill, that we shall pay any price, bear any burden, meet any hardship, support any friend, oppose any foe, to assure the survival and the success of liberty.*

Now we are engaged in a great civil war, testing whether that nation, or any nation so conceived and so dedicated, can long endure. We are met on a great battlefield of that war. We have come to dedicate a portion of that field, as a final resting place for those who here gave their lives that that nation might live. It is altogether fitting and proper that we should do this. [2] *The future doesn't belong to the fainthearted; it belongs to the brave.*

But, in a larger sense, we cannot dedicate—we cannot consecrate—we cannot hallow—this ground. [3] *I have nothing to offer but blood, toil, tears, and sweat.* The brave men, living and dead, who struggled here, have consecrated it, far above our poor power to add or detract. The world will little note, nor long remember what we say here, but it can never forget what they did here. [4] *We hold these truths to be self-evident, that all men are created equal, that they are endowed by their Creator with certain unalienable rights, that among these are life, liberty and the pursuit of happiness.* It is for us the living, rather, to be dedicated here to the unfinished work which they who fought here have thus far so nobly advanced. It is rather for us to be here dedicated to the great task remaining before us—that from these honored dead we take increased devotion to that cause for which they gave the last full measure of devotion—that we here highly resolve that these dead shall not have died in vain—that this nation, under God, shall have a new birth of freedom—and that government of the people, by the people, for the people, shall not perish from the earth. [5] *The only thing we have to fear is fear itself.*

The italicized text in Box 2.2 is from (1) John F. Kennedy's Inaugural Address, 1961; (2) Ronald Reagan's Address to the Nation on the Challenger Space Shuttle Disaster, 1986; (3) Winston Churchill's first speech before the House of Commons after being appointed Prime Minister, 1940; (4) The Declaration of Independence, 1776; and (5) Franklin Delano Roosevelt's First Inaugural Address, 1932. As you read through this version again, note how each of these added sentences moves the text away from Lincoln's thesis—the nation must ensure that the soldiers buried in the National Cemetery of Gettysburg did not die in vain—and how they break the unity of Lincoln's message.

This example notwithstanding, well-written sentences are easier to organize into unified paragraphs because you can more readily determine which sentences support which topic sentences, and how those supporting sentences need to be organized within the paragraph. With poorly written sentences, it is not always clear what they are saying and, hence, what they are supporting.

Renovation Tip

Imagine your paragraph as a herd of cattle (your sentences), with you as the ever-vigilant cowhand (writer) charged with keeping the herd together. Cattle that drift off must be brought back to the herd (the paragraph), while those straying into the herd from other herds (other paragraphs) must be returned. By checking the brand (determining how each sentence is implicitly labeled by the topic sentence it supports), you can identify where all the cattle belong, ensuring every herd stays unified.

Stay Coherent

As well as being unified, paragraphs must be coherent: sentences should build upon one another so naturally that it is obvious how they connect and why one follows the other. "Even if every sentence in a text is crisp, lucid, and well formed," says Steven Pinker in *The Sense of Style: The Thinking Person's Guide to Writing in the 21st Century*, "a *succession* of them can feel choppy, disjointed, unfocused—in a word, incoherent."[2]

It is useful to continually ask: What can I edit, add, delete, or reposition to improve coherence and create the kind of continuity where each sentence in the paragraph flows logically and linguistically into another?

In the following example, the paragraph is unified insofar as everything supports the topic sentence, but the paragraph lacks coherence because the sentences are not aptly related. The result is a paragraph whose sentences do not play together as a team.

ORIGINAL   The University will require all students to take three, two-unit physical activity courses. Next fall will be when it will take place. Denunciation best describes the immediate reaction of students when they heard about this. The fact that students should not be required by the University to play games was the major student complaint. There are exceptions: students over 35 and veterans who have returned from military service will be exempt. The activity courses will replace six units of current General Education requirements. Exemption requests from computer jocks will be handled on a case-by-case basis. Students having senior standing in the fall do not need to worry because they are also exempt from the new requirement.

Placing these sentences into a list underscores the incoherence of the paragraph.

1. The University will require all students to take three, two-unit physical activity courses.

2. Next fall will be when it will take place.

3. Denunciation best describes the immediate reaction of students when they heard about this.

4. The fact that students should not be required by the University to play games was the major student complaint.

5. There are exceptions: students over 35 and veterans who have returned from military service will be exempt.

6. The activity courses will replace six units of current General Education requirements.

7. Exemption requests from computer jocks will be handled on a case-by-case basis.

8. Students having senior standing in the fall do not need to worry because they are also exempt from the new requirement.

Now, let's revise.

Effective next fall,

1. ~~T~~[t]he University will require all students to take three, two-unit physical activity courses.

2. ~~Next fall will be when it will take place.~~

Immediately, students denounced the new policy.

3. ~~Denunciation best describes the immediate reaction of students when they heard about this.~~

They complained they

4. ~~The fact that students~~ should not be required by the University to play games.~~was the major student complaint.~~

Some students, however, will be exempted, including anyone

5. ~~There are exceptions: Students,~~ over 35, ~~and~~ veterans who have returned from military service, ~~will be exempt.~~

2.

6. The[*se*] activity courses will replace six units of current General Education requirements. *(move up to become sentence #2)*

6.

7. Exemption requests from computer jocks will be handled on a case-by-case basis.

and those

8. ~~Students~~ having senior standing in the fall. ~~do not need to worry because they are also exempt from the new requirement.~~

The final, paragraph version:

REVISION   Effective next fall, the University will require all students to take three, two-unit physical activity courses. These activity courses will replace six units of current General Education requirements. Immediately, students denounced the new policy. They complained they should not be required by the University to play games. Some students, however, will be exempted, including anyone over 35, veterans who have returned from military service, and those having senior standing in the fall. Exemption requests from computer jocks will be handled on a case-by-case basis.

The lack of paragraph coherence is what usually betrays the student plagiarist. Long before Turnitin and other similar-type services were available, faculty had little difficulty detecting plagiarized papers. It was not just what the student stole that alerted the professor, but, rather, what the student wrote alongside the lifted material. The inconsistency of the two texts—one having a coherence characterized by elegant, intertwined sentences skillfully punctuated; the other defined by awkwardly worded, oddly sequenced sentences poorly punctuated—revealed the presence of either two writers or one multiple-personality author. Faculty chose to believe it was the former.

A major cause of incoherence is the awkwardly worded sentence, which often reflects a lack of parallel structure. More than just distorting the rhythm of the sentence, nonparallel elements are harder to process because they do not flow smoothly. In the examples that follow, the original version veers off course, leading to an inconsistent grammatical structure that hampers the sentence's readability. The revision corrects the problem by keeping the structure (and meaning) in harmony.

ORIGINAL   Yvone was attracted to Wayne because he excelled at singing, dancing, and had very good knowledge about how to write. She also admired his kindness, sincerity, and that he was generous.

REVISION   Yvone was attracted to Wayne because he excelled at singing, dancing, and writing. She also admired his kindness, sincerity, and generosity.

ORIGINAL   Wayne was attracted to Yvone because she wrote best-selling novels, spoke five languages, was someone who loved fine chocolate, and had ownership of an online editing service.

REVISION   Wayne was attracted to Yvone because she wrote best-selling novels, spoke five languages, loved fine chocolate, and owned an online editing service.

ORIGINAL   Although he was interested in Yvone, Wayne also faced mounting punctuation problems with his latest manuscript, so he pondered: Should I date her or be hiring her?

REVISION   Although he was interested in Yvone, Wayne also faced mounting punctuation problems with his latest manuscript, so he pondered: Should I date her or hire her?

ORIGINAL   Meanwhile, Yvone wondered whether Wayne was simply uninterested in her, or work just preoccupied him.

REVISION   Meanwhile, Yvone wondered whether Wayne was uninterested in her or just preoccupied with work.

ORIGINAL   Yvone decided she would take matters into her own hands and invite Wayne to either a picnic at the park or have lunch at the beach.

REVISION   Yvone decided she would take things into her own hands and invite Wayne to either a picnic at the park or a lunch at the beach.

ORIGINAL   Simultaneously, Wayne had an epiphany: Not experiencing love would be worse than if you had the experience but then lost it.

REVISION   Simultaneously, Wayne had an epiphany: It would be better to have loved and lost than never to have loved at all.

The more organized your thinking, the more coherent your writing. Having strong organizational skills (discussed later in the chapter) allows you to coherently select, order, and connect your ideas/arguments.

You can also enhance paragraph (and page) coherence by providing cues in the form of linguistic labels (identifiers) that aid readers to understand what you are doing and where you are going.

LABEL YOUR THESIS. *My thesis is . . . , My paper argues . . . , This report describes . . . , This e-mail outlines . . . , I contend . . . , I propose . . .* All are ways of identifying your thesis and aiding the reader in comprehending your message. Labeling your thesis also helps ensure you actually have one. In informal writing, where liberal formatting is more acceptable, writers will sometimes italicize or boldface their thesis statement.

LABEL YOUR IDEAS/ARGUMENTS. *Foremost, the coach should be fired because . . . , Another reason why the coach should be fired . . . ,* or *Too, the coach . . .* are examples of how you can label your ideas/arguments. Other words you can use to signal the introduction of a new idea/argument include *additionally, also, and, besides, beyond, finally, further, furthermore, in addition, likewise,* and *moreover.* You can also label ideas/arguments using *first, second,* and *third,* or you can mark them numerically or alphabetically: *1, 2, 3; (a), (b), (c).* Again, if the venue permits, you can italicize, boldface, or bullet each of your main ideas/main arguments.

LABEL YOUR COMPARISONS, CONTRASTS, AND CONNECTIONS. Readers will follow your message more easily if you reinforce important comparisons and contrasts with transitions, such as *although, as opposed to, identical to, in contrast to, however, meanwhile, much like, on the other hand, rather than, similarly, so too, whereas,* and *yet.* You can emphasize connections between ideas/arguments by using such bridging words and phrases as *accordingly, as a result, as such, consequently, hence, so, subsequently, this is why, therefore,* and *thus.*

LABEL KEY SUMMARIES. Label and reinforce summary-type sentences with words and phrases like *generally, in brief, in conclusion, in other words, in short, in sum, in summary,* and *overall.*

Strategic redundancy is yet another way of effecting coherency. Particularly at the end of longer messages, it is helpful to remind readers of your thesis and supporting main ideas/main arguments. Restating them in your conclusion drives home your message. (If your text is short enough or mainly a narrative, a summary usually is not needed.) You can also summarize at the beginning of your message with a *preview* (a summary statement of the main ideas/main arguments you will present), as well as later in your message with an *internal summary* (a review of the main ideas/main arguments you have covered so far). A preview statement can even follow a topic sentence when the intricacy of the paragraph warrants a map of its structure.

Some writers, overestimating their audience's ability to follow message content, give short shrift to labeling and strategic redundancy. They know their message so well they are unaware of how much they subvocalize, especially in terms of omitting helpful linkages and summations from their writing. The absence of such can make even a well-organized message harder to follow.

Others believe that labeling and strategic redundancy will come across as speaking down to their audience. But it is never coherence that audiences resent; it is smugness and deception. Readers welcome writers who take the extra steps to ensure comprehension of their messages. No one ever complains, *The message was much too easy to follow. I prefer when it's more confusing and harder to grasp.* Pinker concludes:

> There is a big difference between a coherent passage of writing and a flaunting of one's erudition, a running journal of one's thoughts, or a published version of one's notes. A coherent text is a designed object: an ordered tree of sections within sections, crisscrossed by arcs that track topics, points, actors, and themes, and held together by connectors that tie one proposition to the next. Like other designed objects, it comes about not by accident but by drafting a blueprint, attending to details, and maintaining a sense of harmony and balance.[3]

Worry Not about Paragraph Length

Theoretically, a paragraph can be any length; there is no minimum or maximum word requirement. But exceptionally long paragraphs, even when devoted to one main idea/main argument, can be challenging to read because they do not provide any visual break in the form of white space

> ## *Renovation Tip*
>
> To assess whether your paragraph is unified and coherent, randomly rearrange the paragraph's sentences and ask a classmate to reassemble them. Does the classmate's reassembled paragraph mirror yours? What would your classmate edit, add, or delete to give the paragraph more unity and coherence? You can use this same approach to test the larger organization of your paper. Select any series of paragraphs, reorder them randomly, and observe how someone else would sequence them. Keep in mind that creating paragraph unity and coherence is easier said than done. Both skills are among the more difficult to master even for accomplished writers.

that permits readers to pause, catch their breath, and mentally refresh. Although long paragraphs may require breaking, short paragraphs do not warrant expanding just because they are short. A paragraph should be as long as is necessary to develop its main idea/main argument.

News stories, feature stories, in-depth pieces, and editorials frequently employ one- and two-sentence paragraphs. This makes sense given the nature of journalism, which, in contrast to other literary forms, tends to abstract main ideas/main arguments. The convention of short paragraphs in print journalism initially grew out of the need to conform to the traditional layout of newspapers (narrow columns), where long paragraphs were harder to read, and where short paragraphs also facilitated the easy cutting of copy when necessary. In today's digital journalism, which places a premium on the speed of story production, short paragraphs, insofar as they compartmentalize thought, allow for quicker editorial decisions about what to keep and what to cut.

In more formal writing, especially in thesis-driven papers, one-sentence paragraphs are less prevalent because the main ideas/main arguments typically require more space to develop. When one- and two-sentence paragraphs do appear in academic writing, they frequently take the form of a preview or summary-type sentence that introduces or concludes an idea/argument having multiple parts.

Beyond its commercial success and critical acclaim—winning seven Academy Awards, including top honors for Best Picture, Best Director, and Best Actor—*The Bridge on the River Kwai* remains a haunting experience because of its intriguing characters and unique plot, its multiple and constantly shifting perspectives, and, of course, its somewhat ambiguous ending. [Subsequent paragraphs develop these arguments.]

The one-sentence paragraph can also emphasize contradiction, contrast, and irony. After listing all the new courses your department said it would schedule, you follow with this one-sentence paragraph: *Three years later, not one of these courses has ever been offered.* After describing the glamorous life of a star college basketball player, you follow with this one-sentence paragraph: *Meanwhile, most of his former high school teammates are back living at home, facing unemployment, and looking for a break.* After detailing how you study all the time while your roommate never even fakes opening a book, you follow with this one-sentence paragraph: *Yet, incredibly, my roommate is seen as a potential Rhodes Scholar.*

Moving from Paragraphs to Pages

All writing, as noted earlier, represents an act of persuasion. By the same token, all writing also informs. Thus, it is useful to categorize messages along the lines of an informative–persuasive continuum that allows for distinguishing between those that seek *primarily to inform* through description and explanation versus those that seek *primarily to persuade* through arguments (conclusions supported by evidence and reasoning) designed to posit, strengthen, or change audience values and beliefs.

Regardless of where your message falls on the informative–persuasive continuum, your first task as a writer is to ask: What is the most important thing I want my audience to know or do? Put another way, if my audience were to read only one sentence of my entire message, what sentence would I choose? The answer is your purpose statement, which is more commonly referred to as your *thesis*. In a single sentence, it conveys the essence, or gist, of what you are asking of your reader.

How you conceptualize and then word your thesis is crucial. Your thesis governs your decision-making about the paragraphs and pages that follow, guiding you in choosing and shaping their content. In cases where messages misconnect with their readers, a main contributing factor is often the writer's failure to present a thesis that overviews and unites the text; or the thesis mischaracterizes the essence of the text and misdirects the reader about what to expect. Worded properly, your thesis helps you to organize your material and stay focused; worded poorly, it runs the risk of confusing, or even losing, your reader before you start.

Although many writers initially think they know what they want to say, often it is only when forced to summarize their purpose into a thesis statement that they realize they have not sufficiently thought through their ideas/arguments. Only then, after critically re-examining and re-evaluating their values and beliefs, do they come to discover what they specifically want to say and why. The revised ideas/arguments that emerge from this exploration reflect the transformative function of the writing process.

Craft Your Thesis Statement

Good thesis statements meet the following five criteria:

1. Your thesis statement should specifically and precisely summarize the goal of your message. If it just introduces your topic, the reader is given little sense of your purpose. You must specifically and precisely forecast what you are about to describe/explain or argue.

ORIGINAL   This paper deals with our dress code.

REVISION A This paper reviews the 15 rules of our dress code. (informative)

REVISION B This paper describes the proposed changes to our dress code. (informative)

ORIGINAL   Something needs to be done about our dress code.

REVISION A The proposed changes to our dress code would result in less productivity. (persuasive)

REVISION B Our dress code should be revised to prevent employees from wearing jumpsuits. (persuasive)

2. Your thesis statement, especially in a persuasive message, should express a sense of conviction and confidence. Trying to render your thesis more palatable by softening its presentation with wimpy wording will merely result in your being seen as weak and uncertain.

ORIGINAL   We should consider revising our dress code.

REVISION   We should revise our dress code. (persuasive)

ORIGINAL   Our dress code may have a problem relative to productivity.

REVISION   Our dress code fails to promote productivity. (persuasive)

Your sense of conviction and confidence, however, should not extend to coloring the wording of your thesis with charged language that assumes the acceptance of arguments you have yet to make.

ORIGINAL   We should revise our silly dress code.

REVISION   We should revise our dress code. (persuasive)

ORIGINAL   Our outdated dress code fails to promote productivity.

REVISION   Our dress code fails to promote productivity. (persuasive)

You can argue the dress code should be revised *because* it is silly, or the dress code does not promote productivity *because* it is outdated. But these arguments must be developed, not presupposed. Your thesis should be worded in a way that does not give unfair advantage to someone arguing either for or against it.

3. Your thesis statement should be succinct and not overly detailed. Long thesis statements overcrowded with information can be hard to process. Generally, for example, your thesis statement should not include a preview of your supporting main ideas/main arguments, which can lead to an unwieldy statement that overwhelms the reader. Instead, keep your thesis statement separate and then follow up, if necessary, with a preview statement.

ORIGINAL   The Piranha Rescue Habitat will hold a manager's workshop to discuss how to recruit new employees from three sectors—private, nonprofit, and government—and will include a discussion of which print, electronic, and digital media outlets to use for advertising; how to analyze traditional and digital resumés; and what types of closed and open-ended questions to ask in interviews [thesis statement combined with preview statement].

REVISION   The Piranha Rescue Habitat will hold a manager's workshop to discuss how to recruit new employees [thesis statement]. The workshop will include (1) where to advertise the position, (2) how to analyze different types of resumés, and (3) what questions to ask in job interviews [preview statement].

Occasionally, you can join your thesis and preview if the combined statement remains short enough. You can then follow up with a more detailed preview that foreshadows the substructure of the ideas/arguments to come.

ORIGINAL   Professor Hehl should be fired because he is disorganized in his lectures, presentation slides, and online materials; he tests unfairly, whether the examination is essay, short answer, or multiple choice; and he abhors research and researchers, regardless of their discipline or methodological approach [thesis statement with detailed preview].

REVISION   Professor Hehl should be fired because he is disorganized, tests unfairly, and abhors research [thesis statement with brief preview]. More specifically, I will argue that (1) he is disorganized in three areas of teaching—his lectures, presentation slides, and online materials; (2) he tests unfairly, whether the examination is essay, short answer, or multiple choice; and (3) he abhors research and researchers, regardless of their discipline or methodological approach [detailed preview].

Nor should your thesis statement summarize "the how" when you are describing an existing policy or proposing a new one. The how can certainly be part of your message, but it is not normally part of your thesis statement.

ORIGINAL   Rite University teaches writing across the curriculum by training all professors, via on-campus and online workshops taught by campus experts, on how to evaluate writing and how to include writing assignments in all their courses, whether they be lower division, upper division, or graduate level.

REVISION   Rite University teaches writing across the curriculum. (informative)

ORIGINAL   The company should prohibit employees from wearing flip-flops during normal business hours by changing the rules of the Employee Handbook and then posting signs throughout the building that read, *Real Employees Wear Real Shoes.*

REVISION   The company should prohibit employees from wearing flip-flops during normal business hours. (persuasive)

4. Your thesis statement should be worded as a short, declarative sentence, not as a question. A declarative sentence immediately states your position; a question does not.

ORIGINAL   How do employees feel about the new rule against interoffice dating?

REVISION   Most employees like the new rule against interoffice dating. (informative)

ORIGINAL   Does the University have the right to raise tuition every month?

REVISION A The University has the right to raise tuition every month. (persuasive)

REVISION B The University does not have the right to raise tuition every month. (persuasive)

5. Your thesis statement should contain one central idea/central argument, not two or three. A thesis statement having more than one central idea/central argument means you have more than one thesis. This can confuse your reader, who must reconcile two or more different sets of supporting ideas/supporting arguments brought together in service of two or more different purposes. Because it is easier to process one central idea/central argument at a time, unrelated purposes should be addressed separately.

ORIGINAL   I will describe the University's new requirement that all students be proficient in three languages, as well as explain the University's tuition refund policy for students who drop out before the second week of classes.

REVISION A I will describe the University's new requirement that all students be proficient in three languages. (informative)

REVISION B I will explain the University's tuition refund policy for students who drop out before the second week of classes. (informative)

ORIGINAL   The company should extend the lunch break to two hours and provide stock options to all employees.

REVISION A The company should extend the lunch break to two hours. (persuasive)

REVISION B The company should provide stock options to all employees. (persuasive)

If you have several closely related ideas/arguments, try subsuming them under one overarching central idea/central argument, represented by your thesis statement.

ORIGINAL   The Journalism Department should hire more new media faculty, offer additional courses in social media writing, broaden its internship partnerships with local media, and establish a tutorial center for majors [thesis statement].

The statement presents several arguments without any unifying thread showing how they relate or how they are subordinate to a larger, central argument (your thesis).

REVISION   The Journalism Department should significantly change how it teaches classes and mentors students [thesis statement]. [You then follow up with a preview of the four proposed changes:] More specifically, the Journalism Department should hire more new media faculty, offer additional courses in social media writing, broaden its internship partnerships with local media, and establish a tutorial center for majors.

(Note that *teaches classes and mentors students* are so closely related they are treated as one, not two, ideas, in the same way that *cruel and unusual* is treated as a singular idea.)

You may not know your exact purpose until you have sorted out your entire message. Viewing all your ideas/arguments at once can help you apprehend the thesis that unites them. In the example above, the act of first listing everything wrong with the Journalism Department facilitates the process of synthesis, making it easier to conclude, *The Journalism Department should significantly change how it teaches classes and mentors students.*

When you are unsure of your purpose, starting with a tentative thesis statement can help you work through your message and figure out exactly what you want to say, which then leads to a refining of your thesis statement. It is also wise to reconsider your thesis statement *after* you have finished drafting your message. Questions similar to the ones you would ask in evaluating your topic sentence should be posed: Does my thesis statement encompass all the main ideas/main arguments presented in my message? If not, can it be revised accordingly, or must I revise my main ideas/main arguments to fit my thesis statement?

Position Your Thesis Statement

Your thesis statement should appear in your paper's introduction, usually in the first paragraph. It may be the lead sentence of the paragraph, or it may come later in the paragraph should brief, contextual background information first be needed. If you have a lot of background material that is helpful but not crucial to understanding your message, place it after your opening paragraph so as not to sidetrack your reader with an initial barrage of detail. Near or at the end of your paper's introduction, it is a good idea to preview your message. Note: In longer reports and academic papers, your thesis statement may appear in the last paragraph of a multi-paragraph introduction, especially if it is essential to first establish the relevance and significance of your subject. Regardless of the length of your introduction, it houses your thesis statement.

Stating your thesis in the first paragraph increases the chances it will be read. Although readers often skim and skip message content, they usually read all or most of the first paragraph. Knowing your thesis from the start gives your audience an immediate point of reference for everything that follows; it foretells where you are going and how it is all connected. Conversely, when you build to your thesis, your message is harder to track because your audience must connect the dots along the way. Readers who tire of the extra work may not stick around.

Nonfiction writing is sometimes composed as if it were a dramatic story. The author creates suspense, holding back the thesis statement until the end. If you are writing a mystery, this makes sense. You introduce clues (evidence) throughout the story and then reveal the murderer (the conclusion) in the closing pages. Mystery readers enjoy the leisurely challenge of identifying the culprit because it is how they are entertained. In our everyday routines, however, we often have too much to read in too little time; we are not amused by detective work. From the classroom to the boardroom, we first want to know: *Who is the murderer?* Beforehand, we need to be told what the evidence will prove.

Why, then, is so much writing organized backward, the writer failing to first state his/her thesis? Perhaps it is because most research follows a *climactic* pattern: you collect pieces of information (data) and then look to see what conclusion they support. The mistake is following the same

Renovation Tip

A climactic writing pattern may be appropriate for announcing "bad" news, such as laying off an employee, canceling the holiday party, or disclosing you just dropped out of school. In these cases, starting with your thesis statement—*Pack up your bags, you're no longer part of the team; Sorry, but we're not celebrating any holidays this year; Dear Mom and Dad, I left school yesterday and will be joining a carnival tomorrow*—can cast you as cold and insensitive, worsening an already trying situation. A climactic approach prepares the audience for the bad news by leading up to it.

climactic pattern—starting with data and then building toward a conclusion (your central idea/central argument worded as a thesis)—when you write.

Ordinarily, most nonfiction messages should be organized *anti-climactically*: your thesis comes before its supporting data. Inverting the steps of your research process, you begin with your conclusion before explaining how you got there. Organizing your writing this way makes it easier to read.

Position Your Supporting Ideas/Arguments

Following your introduction, the body of your message reintroduces and develops the main ideas/main arguments that support your thesis, which, in turn, are supported by evidence (facts/statistics, examples, and testimony).

In shorter papers, a main idea/main argument can usually be developed in a single paragraph. For longer papers whose main ideas/main arguments have extensive substructure, several paragraphs may be required to cover each main idea/main argument. These paragraphs usually will address *subideas* or *subarguments* that together support or comprise the larger main idea/main argument. In other words, just as each of your paragraphs must be unified and coherent, so, too, must they collectively forge a unified and coherent whole that supports your thesis.

Consider this example: *John should not be elected student body president* [thesis] *because he is dishonest, cannot manage, and is emotionally unstable* [preview of three main arguments combined into thesis statement]. If you were to find substantial evidence that *John is dishonest* and that his dishonesty takes three distinct forms—lying, stealing, and cheating—each subargument (*John lies, John steals, John cheats*) could then be developed in one or more paragraphs.

Sometimes you may need to structurally break down an argument even further. If you were to say that John lies by commission (what he says) and omission (what he does not say), you would have two sub-subarguments—*John lies by commission* and *John lies by omission*—falling under the subargument *John lies*. Again, you could develop each of these subarguments in one or more paragraphs. The primary idea/argument the paragraph addresses, regardless of its structural level, always represents the paragraph's *bottom line*, expressed by the paragraph's topic sentence.

The topic sentence, as earlier noted, commonly appears as the first sentence of the paragraph. Frequently, however, writers will choose, without apparent reason, to lead up to the topic sentence, or, worse, embed it in the middle of the paragraph. In these cases, the topic sentence needs to be extracted and repositioned as the paragraph's first sentence. The two examples that follow, of an informative message and a persuasive message, illustrate how you would normally position bottomlined ideas/arguments as topic sentences.

If you were informing readers of your company's new process for travel reimbursement, you could start with something like this:

1ST PARAGRAPH

This e-mail describes the three steps involved in our new Travel Reimbursement Procedure when staying at beachfront destinations [thesis statement]. These steps include (1) getting your supervisor's approval before taking the trip, (2) completing our new travel reimbursement form upon your return, and (3) attaching all travel receipts to the form [preview].

In terms of background information, this paragraph could briefly include what motivated the change in policy and when it took effect.

Each subsequent paragraph would advance the thesis statement by developing one of its supporting main ideas. Paragraphs two, three, and four would begin with topic sentences that bottomline steps 1, 2, and 3, respectively, with the rest of the paragraph elaborating upon each step. Your topic (first) sentences might read:

2ND PARAGRAPH

FIRST SENTENCE The first and most important step in the new Travel Reimbursement Procedure is making sure you have your supervisor's approval before taking your trip.

3RD PARAGRAPH

FIRST SENTENCE You will also need to complete the new travel reimbursement form upon your return.

4TH PARAGRAPH

FIRST SENTENCE The final step in the new procedure requires you to attach all travel receipts to the form.

Now, let's look at a persuasive message and return to *John should not be elected student body president*. After an introductory paragraph that introduces this thesis, your main arguments would appear in the body of your message, bottomlined with topic sentences.

2ND PARAGRAPH

FIRST SENTENCE Foremost, John should not be elected student body president because he is dishonest.

3RD PARAGRAPH

FIRST SENTENCE Another reason why John should not be elected is that he cannot manage.

4TH PARAGRAPH

FIRST SENTENCE If being dishonest and a poor manager were not enough, John is also emotionally unstable.

Effectively introducing your thesis and then clearly structuring its supporting ideas/arguments can sometimes be a matter of just repositioning your thesis statement, re-paragraphing your text, and adding a few words to help guide the reader. In the example below, neither the writer's thesis nor its supporting arguments are highlighted. Instead, all are combined into one paragraph without obvious differentiation.

ORIGINAL

I'd like to discuss the matter of staff support in our office. For many months now, the Center for Effective and Efficient Management has been short-staffed, which has led to its deteriorating performance. The Center has become inefficient. Clients should not have to wait a week or longer, as they do now, before hearing from us. We need to answer client questions about our consulting services promptly. The Center has become unprofessional. Our work product is often messy and incomplete. I know that the staff is stretched too far and does not have time to carefully prepare and edit e-mails and letters to clients. However, a poor work product reflects negatively on our image. It is not good for business. The cost of hiring more staff will be offset by the financial benefits of reestablishing our clients' trust and confidence. Many of our clients are starting to go elsewhere for our services, as shown by last quarter's decline in sales. I propose we hire at least three new employees.

A revision of this example starts by deleting the first sentence, which masquerades as a thesis statement, albeit a poor one that has no point of view and says little. The actual thesis statement coming at the end of the message—*I propose we hire at least three new employees*—is then moved to what becomes the first paragraph. Labeling each main argument and placing it into a new, bottomlined paragraph drives home the message. (underlined text = added copy)

REVISION

~~I'd like to discuss the matter of staff support in our office.~~ For many months now, the Center for Effective and Efficient Management has been short-staffed, which has led to its deteriorating performance. To remedy the problem, I propose we hire at least three new employees. More specifically, here's why:

First, the Center has become inefficient. Clients should not have to wait a week or longer, as they do now, before hearing from us. We need to answer client questions about our consulting services promptly.

Second, the Center has become unprofessional. Our work product is often messy and incomplete. I know that the staff is stretched too far and does not have time to carefully prepare and edit e-mails and letters to clients. However, a poor work product reflects negatively on our image. It is not good for business.

Finally, the cost of hiring more staff will be offset by the financial benefits of reestablishing our clients' trust and confidence. Many of our clients are starting to go elsewhere for our services, as shown by last quarter's decline in sales.

Structure Your Supporting Ideas/Arguments, Part I

When you present a well-structured idea/argument, you enhance its strength and readability. As James B. Stewart notes in *Follow the Story: How to Write Successful Nonfiction*:

> The presence of structure reassures readers that they are in the hands of a skilled storyteller, someone they can trust with their time and interest. They know they are going somewhere, which means they can relax and enjoy the journey.[4]

Longer works, including many academic papers, can be challenging to structure when they feature complex and interrelated ideas/arguments. Effective organization usually requires breaking down main ideas/main arguments into a structural hierarchy that includes subideas/subarguments, sub-subideas/sub-subarguments, and beyond if necessary. Although this pre-writing process can be tedious and time-consuming, it pays big dividends: in addition to maximizing the readability and appeal of your message, pre-writing facilitates write-ability (i.e., it is easier and faster to write any paper once you know where all the pieces fit).

Let's return to *John should not be elected student body president.* Assume you have a large arsenal of proof, sixteen pieces of evidence to be exact, showing John to be dishonest in various ways. You could simply present one piece after another, lumping all without any thematic organization represented by substructure. However, this approach—treating the evidence discretely rather than holistically—would not connect the evidence in ways that shepherd the reader in its processing. Moreover, the writer who abandons substructure also surrenders the opportunity to create more substantial main ideas and more compelling main arguments (e.g., John is not *just* dishonest; he is dishonest in *three* different ways).

The process of substructuring main ideas/main arguments begins by grouping and naming similar-themed pieces of evidence based on the features they have in common. In the case of *John should not be elected student body president,* you would first need to identify and label the type of dishonesty—lying (El), cheating (Ec), or stealing (Es)—each piece of evidence supports.

Es	Ec	El	Es
El	Ec	Es	El
Ec	El	Ec	Es
El	Es	El	Ec

Now, organize the evidence into themed subpiles and name the subpiles using short, parallel-structured (when possible), complete sentences that capture the conclusion each subpile supports.

Subpile 1: El, El, El, El, El, El   =   *John lies.* (subargument A)

Subpile 2: Ec, Ec, Ec, Ec, Ec   =   *John cheats.* (subargument B)

Subpile 3: Es, Es, Es, Es, Es   =   *John steals.* (subargument C)

Using this framework, the paragraphs following the introduction of your thesis (*John should not be elected student body president*) might look something like this:

2ND PARAGRAPH

IN ENTIRETY   Foremost, John should not be elected student body president because he is dishonest. This dishonesty takes several forms.

3RD PARAGRAPH

FIRST SENTENCE   John lies habitually. (followed by evidence: El, El, El, El, El, El)

4TH PARAGRAPH

FIRST SENTENCE   John also cheats whenever he gets the chance. (followed by evidence: Ec, Ec, Ec, Ec, Ec)

5TH PARAGRAPH

FIRST SENTENCE   Yet another way John is dishonest is that he steals. (followed by evidence: Es, Es, Es, Es, Es)

The naming of piles, subpiles, sub-subpiles, and beyond provides the core wording for the subsequent, usually somewhat more extended, introduction of your ideas/arguments in your paper. The very process of summarizing your ideas/arguments into short, parallel-structured, complete sentences also helps you to grasp the essence of what you want to say, which, in turn, makes it easier to compare your ideas/arguments and judge how well they organizationally relate and come together in support of larger ideas/arguments.

Subideas/subarguments, as discussed, essentially break down your main ideas/main arguments into related parts around which it is easier to organize your evidence and build your paragraphs. The same process by which you arrive at your subideas/subarguments also comes into play earlier when you first analyze all your evidence to determine the main ideas/main arguments it supports. In the case of *John should not be elected student body president*, you would have concluded it falls into three themed piles: John is dishonest, John cannot manage, and John is emotionally unstable. Simply put, the evidence forms bodies of support for broad conclusions, which become your main ideas/main arguments. How your evidence shapes the formation and wording of your main ideas/main arguments, subideas/subarguments, and beyond can be further seen in this example of an informative message describing the ways an earthquake adversely affected one family:

1. The garage roof collapsed.
2. I fractured my right index finger.
3. Our desktop computer broke into 86 pieces.
4. Our killer shark aquarium now leaks in three places.
5. Several of our clothes fell off their hangers.
6. The head of our favorite Elvis statue was demolished.
7. The frame broke on the largest of our Lady Gaga velvet paintings.
8. Our cat sprained her left foot.
9. The wall-to-wall shag carpet was stained in several places.
10. Our dog chipped a tooth.
11. The wedding pictures from my sixth marriage burst into flames.
12. My notes from my first college composition class were thrown about my study.
13. My husband suffered a separated shoulder.
14. The main gas line snapped.
15. The wooden patio doors were scratched.

Organizing this evidence begins, as always, with the grouping of pieces that share obvious commonalities. From there, you work your way down, refining the organizational piles into subpiles, sub-subpiles, and beyond. Start by asking: Of the listed items, which are similar in nature? Obviously, some are living objects (people and pets), while others are inanimate objects of various sorts. The living:

2. I fractured my right index finger.

8. Our cat sprained her left foot.

10. Our dog chipped a tooth.

13. My husband suffered a separated shoulder.

These four pieces of evidence go into a pile, which you name *The earthquake injured family members.* But wait, can we break this pile into two subpiles? After all, the earthquake injured two different life forms: humans and pets. Wouldn't it be better to discuss human injuries before pet injuries? Following your first paragraph and the introduction of your thesis—*The earthquake adversely affected our family*—your second paragraph might look like this:

2ND PARAGRAPH

[1st of paper's three main ideas:] Foremost, the earthquake injured family members. [1st subidea, People were injured:] My husband suffered a separated shoulder, which was very painful and took three months to heal. I fractured my right index finger and was unable to pitch in my Over-75 Super Senior Softball League. [2nd subidea, Pets were injured:] Meanwhile, our pets endured injuries as well. Maria, our cat, sprained her left foot and has been unable to catch mice for weeks. Our beautiful show dog, Victoria, chipped a tooth and will need dental work before she can compete again.

Although the remaining pile of evidence is quite large, four items clearly reference house damage:

1. The garage roof collapsed.

9. The wall-to-wall shag carpet was stained in several places.

14. The main gas line snapped.

15. The wooden patio doors were scratched.

The second main pile of evidence can now be named: *The earthquake damaged our house.* To group these four supporting pieces of evidence without distinction, however, would imply all are of equal significance. Breaking the pile into subpiles—major and minor damage—emphasizes the major damage.

3RD PARAGRAPH

[2nd of paper's three main ideas:] Too, the earthquake damaged our house. [1st subidea, Our house sustained major damage:] Major damage included the collapsed garage roof and the snapped main gas line. Estimates to repair the garage roof range from $3000 to $4500. We may incur more costs because the garage will be unprotected from the weather until we repair the roof. Fortunately, the main gas line will not be as expensive to fix as the roof, but it does pose a major danger inasmuch as overworked city repair crews have not had time to replace the line. [2nd subidea, Our house sustained minor damage:] As if all this were not enough, minor damage to the house will add to our cost, time, and inconvenience. We will need to repair the wooden patio doors scratched by a falling tree branch, and we will have to hire a professional to clean the wall-to-wall shag carpet, now stained in several places.

Organizing a paper is somewhat like puzzle-solving: as each piece falls into place, it becomes easier to see where the next one fits. Now with fewer pieces of evidence left to organize, it is evident that what remains describes personal property and includes items that incurred IRREPARABLE DAMAGE, **major damage**, or no damage:

3. OUR DESKTOP COMPUTER BROKE INTO 86 PIECES.

4. **Our killer shark aquarium now leaks in three places.**

5. Several of our clothes fell off their hangers.

6. THE HEAD OF OUR FAVORITE ELVIS STATUE WAS DEMOLISHED.

7. **The frame broke on the largest of our Lady Gaga velvet paintings.**

11. THE WEDDING PICTURES FROM MY SIXTH MARRIAGE BURST INTO FLAMES.

12. My notes from my first college composition class were thrown about my study.

The process of organizing evidence into piles also exposes those ideas/arguments not worth pursuing. To talk of falling clothes and disarrayed class notes in the same breath as damaged personal property runs the risk of trivializing your message and lowering your credibility.

4TH PARAGRAPH

[3rd of paper's three main ideas:] In addition to the toll the earthquake took on our health and home, it also damaged personal property. [1st subidea, Personal property sustained irreparable damage:] Some items incurred irreparable damage, such as our desktop computer, broken into 86 pieces; our favorite Elvis statue, whose head was demolished; and the wedding pictures from my sixth marriage, which burst into flames. [2nd subidea, Personal property sustained major damage:] Other items, such as our killer shark aquarium and the frame on the largest of our Lady Gaga velvet paintings, incurred major damage and will require significant repair.

Renovation Tip

A good test of whether your topic sentences effectively bottomline your main ideas/main arguments is to have someone read the first paragraph of your paper and then just the first sentence of each succeeding paragraph. A well-organized message will make considerable (not complete) sense even after such an abbreviated reading.

Structure Your Supporting Ideas/Arguments, Part II

Knowing how to group and sub-group ideas/arguments and their supporting evidence enables you to produce a detailed outline, which further aids in shaping your message and enhancing its readability and appeal. An effective outline permits you to see how your ideas/arguments and evidence structurally relate and how their presentation should be developed and sequenced. But just having an outline does not necessarily yield a well-structured message. It is the quality of the outline that counts: whether it illuminates the interplay of your thoughts and captures what should be highlighted, downplayed, or eliminated.

Putting together an effective outline is harder than it seems. An outline is not a bulleted list or a list simply prefaced by Roman and Arabic numbers and upper- and lowercase letters. An outline organizes your ideas/arguments and evidence from general to specific, delineating what is *coordinate* and

Box 2.3 *The Earthquake Adversely Affected Our Family*

I.   The earthquake injured family members.   [main idea]

    A. People were injured.   [subidea]
      1. My husband suffered a separated
      shoulder.   [evidence]
      2. I fractured my right index finger.   [evidence]

    B. Pets were injured.   [subidea]
      1. Our cat sprained her left foot.   [evidence]
      2. Our dog chipped a tooth.   [evidence]

II. The earthquake damaged our house.   [main idea]

    A. Our house sustained major damage.   [subidea]
      1. The garage roof collapsed.   [evidence]
      2. The main gas line snapped.   [evidence]

    B. Our house sustained minor damage.   [subidea]
      1. The wooden patio doors were scratched. [evidence]
      2. The upstairs wall-to-wall shag carpet was
      stained in several places.   [evidence]

III. The earthquake damaged personal property.   [main idea]

    A. Personal property sustained irreparable
    damage.   [subidea]
      1. Our desktop house computer broke into
      86 pieces.   [evidence]
      2. The head of our favorite Elvis statue was
      demolished.   [evidence]
      3. The wedding pictures from my sixth
      marriage burst into flames.   [evidence]

    B. Personal property sustained major damage.   [subidea]
      1. Our killer shark aquarium now leaks in
      three places.   [evidence]
      2. The frame broke on the largest of our
      Lady Gaga velvet paintings.   [evidence]

what is *superior*. Ideas/arguments and evidence are coordinate when they provide an equal level of structural support for the superior idea/argument to which they are *subordinate*.

An outline of *The earthquake adversely affected our family* (specifically what would comprise the body of the message) serves as an illustration (Box 2.3). The evidence supports the (superior) subideas; the subideas support the (superior) main ideas; and the main ideas support the (superior) thesis.

Although each main idea (I, II, and III) in this sample outline contains two subideas (A and B), a main idea/main argument may need to be divided into more than two subideas/subarguments, or it may not need to be divided at all. A main idea/main argument, however, cannot be divided into a single subidea/subargument any more than you can "break" a stick into one. If you were to eliminate subidea II,B (*Our house sustained minor damage*), you could not still structure your second main idea this way:

II. The earthquake damaged our house.

    A. Our house sustained major damage.

        1. The garage roof collapsed.

        2. The main gas line snapped.

The single subidea (II,A) adds unnecessary structure that can confuse the reader. *Our house sustained major damage* in this context is not so much a subidea as it is a more precise wording of the main idea. Deleting the subidea and slightly revising the main idea corrects the problem.

II. The earthquake caused major damage to our house.

    A. The garage roof collapsed.

    B. The main gas line snapped.

This revised main idea has no subideas. The two pieces of evidence (now labeled A and B) directly support the main idea.

A main idea/main argument can be substructured only if it yields a minimum of two subideas/subarguments that differ from—but relate to—one another in the sense they both support, but in different ways, the larger idea/argument to which they are subordinate. A roof collapse differs from

Box 2.4

Introduction

I. We are a school with a rich tradition of student governance and student leadership.

    A. Over the years, our student body presidents have contributed positively to the direction of the school.

    B. The most successful presidents were those who had integrity, knew how to manage, and were emotionally stable.

    C. Our next student body president must possess these same qualities if we are to continue our tradition of strong student leadership.

II. *Thesis statement:* John should not be elected student body president.

III. *Preview:* He is dishonest, cannot manage, and is emotionally unstable.

Body

I. John is dishonest.   [main argument]

    A. He lies.   [subargument]
       [evidence]

    B. He cheats.   [subargument]
       [evidence]

    C. He steals.   [subargument]
       [evidence]

II. John cannot manage.   [main argument]

    A. He cannot supervise.   [subargument]
       [evidence]

    B. He cannot organize.   [subargument]
       [evidence]

    C. He cannot prioritize.   [subargument]
       [evidence]

continued

III. John is emotionally unstable. [main argument]

    A. He is irrational. [subargument]
    [evidence]

    B. He is paranoid. [subargument]
    [evidence]

Conclusion

I. Summary of arguments:

    A. He is dishonest.
    B. He cannot manage.
    C. He is emotionally unstable.

II. Repeat thesis statement: John should not be elected student body president.

III. Closing quotation that speaks to the importance of quality leadership.

a snapped main gas line, but both are evidence of how the earthquake caused major damage to the house.

Box 2.4 shows how the introduction, body, and conclusion of *John should not be elected student body president* might be outlined.

Note that the three main arguments why John should not be elected student body president must differ in kind, and they do: dishonesty, poor management skills, and emotional instability represent distinct problems that can exist independently of one another. The main arguments must also share the same overall function, and they do: they all directly support the thesis statement, *John should not be elected student body president.*

Similarly, the subarguments must be both different from, but related to, one another. The subarguments of all three main arguments meet this criterion, starting with the first main argument:

I. John is dishonest.

    A. He lies.
    B. He cheats.
    C. He steals.

Lying, cheating, and stealing are not the same thing: you can engage in one without engaging in all three. All three acts, however, are forms of dishonesty and thereby represent three unique but complementary, coordinate parts of a whole. They coordinate with one another because they are equally subordinate to the superior main point, *John is dishonest,* which they individually and collectively support.

Should you have but one single subargument why John is dishonest (e.g., *He lies*), delete the subargument and reword your main argument to reflect the subargument.

INCORRECT	CORRECT
I. John is dishonest.	**I.** John lies.
A. He lies.	**A.** evidence
1. evidence	**B.** evidence
2. evidence	**C.** evidence
3. evidence	**D.** evidence
4. evidence	

Finally, the wording of each main argument must be broad enough to cover its subordinate parts, yet specific enough to reflect its larger thrust. *John cannot manage,* for example, is a well-worded main argument because it encompasses its three subarguments: to *manage* is to supervise, organize, and prioritize. Other seemingly similar wordings of the main argument would not be as effective. *John cannot boss well* would be too narrowly worded, basically repeating one of the subarguments, *He cannot supervise,* and failing to effectively summarize the other two subarguments, *He cannot organize* and *He cannot prioritize.* On the other hand, *John is incompetent* would be too broad, not specific enough in its summary of what it collectively means when someone cannot supervise, organize, and prioritize (i.e., he/she cannot manage).

Having a large stack of main ideas/main arguments is usually a sure sign you do not have enough subidea/subargument development. What appear to be main ideas/main arguments are more likely to be subideas/subarguments needing to be grouped and subsumed under larger headings. Take the previous example and suppose that instead of three main arguments—*John is dishonest, John cannot manage, and John is emotionally unstable*—you presented eight:

I.   John lies.

II.   John cheats.

III.   John steals.

IV.   John cannot supervise.

V.   John cannot organize.

VI.   John cannot prioritize.

VII.   John is irrational.

VIII.   John is paranoid.

Less reader friendly, this message would have been difficult to process and to remember. The eight main arguments—in contrast to the three arguments advanced with subdevelopment in the sample outline—are not given any structural connection to indicate how they relate to one another. Organizing your message around fewer main ideas/main arguments with subdevelopment facilitates readability and allows you to build better, more mature main ideas/main arguments.

Shaky organization explains why so many messages miss their mark. Extended-length writing, in particular, mandates exceptional organizational skills. Great sentences do not automatically come together to structurally form great paragraphs, and great paragraphs do not necessarily lead to great pages.

Constructing a well-organized message is arduous because we subvocalize so much of our text. Try as we may to critique our own writing, structural flaws can elude us. Adding to the problem, many writers resist starting with an outline because they feel it inhibits their creativity. Yet it is nearly impossible to produce well-organized, longer messages without having a prewriting tool, such as an outline, to guide you at some point in the process.

One solution is a reverse outline: you outline your entire text *after* you complete your first draft. The reverse outline reveals not what you *wanted* to say, but what you *did* say and *where* you said it. When you compare your thesis statement to your main ideas/main arguments, two problems often emerge: (1) A paragraph's main idea/main argument is concurrently developed under another paragraph's main idea/main argument, or it is sporadically developed throughout the text. (2) One or more of what should be a paragraph's subideas/subarguments have migrated to other paragraphs as part of their substructure. When subideas/subarguments roam randomly about your text, readers are sent in too many confusing, disorienting directions.

Note the misplaced arguments and subarguments in Box 2.5.

Box 2.5

I.	John is dishonest.	
	A. He cheats.	
	B. He steals.	
	C. He's unbalanced.	[repeat of main argument III]
II.	John cannot manage.	
	A. He cannot organize.	
	B. He cannot prioritize.	
	C. He lies.	[subargument belonging under main argument I]
	D. He is irrational.	[subargument belonging under main argument III]
III.	John is emotionally unstable.	
	A. He cannot supervise.	[subargument belonging under main argument II]
	B. He is paranoid.	
	C. He's not truthful.	[repeat of main argument I]

Besides pinpointing major organizational problems, a reverse outline can help when you become mired in a writing project, unable to move forward. Outlining what you have completed so far can pinpoint where you are and where you need to go.

"Give me six hours to chop down a tree," Abraham Lincoln is thought to have said, "and I will spend the first four sharpening the axe." The time you devote to outlining and reverse outlining—sharpening your prewriting tools—will more than pay for itself. A quality outline enables you to write more effectively and efficiently.

Renovation Tip

When you write a persuasive message, one way to ensure your arguments are germane is to think of your thesis statement followed by *because*. Read your thesis statement as a preface to each main argument (expressed by a topic sentence) to see whether the argument, as worded, directly supports your thesis: *John should not be elected student body president because . . . he is dishonest.* Yes, this works.

Combining thesis and argument underscores the disconnect when a main argument does not directly support the thesis, as in these examples:

- John should not be elected student body president because . . . honesty should be considered.
- John should not be elected student body president because . . . previous presidents have been honest.
- John should not be elected student body president because . . . the president should not be dishonest.

The three arguments—*honesty should be considered, previous presidents have been honest*, and *the president should not be dishonest*—do not specifically address John's dishonesty. If fact, readers could agree with all three arguments and still believe that John is honest.

The act of grouping items is something most of us are more experienced at than we realize. Take the typical house garage, where it is common to store and organize such items as sports equipment, power tools, gardening equipment and supplies, holiday decorations, and old clothes. As with ideas/arguments, these items can be separated into piles, subpiles, sub-subpiles, and more. Sports equipment, for instance, could be broken into three subpiles, one of which might be baseball (Box 2.6).

Organizing three-dimensional objects is obviously not quite the same as organizing a paper. You can more readily see similarities and differences between familiar objects than you can between sentences. This is true even when the sentences reference objects, let alone when they symbolize more abstract thought, such as values and beliefs.

Box 2.6 *Sports Equipment (pile)*

Baseball (subpile)	Soccer (subpile)	Golf (subpiles)

Gloves (sub-subpile)
    Fielder (sub-sub-subpile)
        Right hand (sub-sub-sub-subpile)
        Left hand (sub-sub-sub-subpile)
    First base
        Right hand
        Left hand
    Catcher
        Right hand
        Left hand

Bats
    Wood
        34 inches
        33 inches
        32 inches
        31 inches
        30 inches
    Aluminum
        34 inches
        33 inches
        32 inches
        31 inches
        30 inches

Balls
    Baseballs
        New
        Used
    Softballs
        New
            11 inches (sub-sub-sub-sub-subpile)

continued

12 inches (sub-sub-sub-sub-subpile)
16 inches (sub-sub-sub-sub-subpile)
Used
11 inches
12 inches
16 inches

Batting gloves
Right hand
Left hand

Batting helmets
With earflaps
Without earflaps

Although it is easier organizing objects, as opposed to thoughts, into piles, both activities share the same goal and analytical process. We organize a garage so we can access whatever we need with minimal effort and frustration. Similarly, we organize messages to facilitate their reading. But unlike when you enter your garage, your readers enter your message with no prior knowledge of what to look for and where to find it. Effective structure guides them in identifying the various elements of your message.

EXERCISES

Exercise 1

In the following passage, Oliver Wendell Holmes, Jr. overviews why we study the law.[5] Which four sentences added from other sources (Benjamin Franklin, Blaise Pascal, Voltaire, and Louis Brandeis) disturb the unity of the paragraph?

When we study law we are not studying a mystery but a well-known profession. Laws too gentle are seldom obeyed; too severe, seldom executed. We are studying what we shall want in order to appear before judges, or to advise people in such a way as to keep them out of court. The reason why it is a profession, why people will pay lawyers to argue for them or to advise them, is that in societies like ours the command of the public force is intrusted to the judges in certain cases, and the whole power of the state will be put forth, if necessary, to carry out their judgments and decrees. Law without force is impotent. People want to know under what circumstances and how far they will run the risk of coming against what is so much stronger than themselves, and hence it becomes a business to find out when this danger is to be feared. It is dangerous to be right on matters on which the established authorities are wrong. The object of our study, then, is prediction, the prediction of the incidence of the public force through the instrumentality of the courts. In a government of laws, existence of the government will be imperiled if it fails to observe the law scrupulously.

Exercise 2

Arrange these sentences into a coherent paragraph that begins with this sentence: *To what extent can criminal trials be expected to establish the truth about historic events for journalists?*[6]

A. In the popular imagination, however, a trial performs a somewhat grander service.

B. In law, the purpose of a criminal trial is to decide, according to predetermined rules, whether a defendant is guilty or not guilty of a particular charge.

C. The general assumption is that, if fairly conducted, a trial will yield the whole truth; aside from meting out justice to the accused, it will provide complete information and resolve the doubts of a concerned public.

D. Adversary proceedings are designed to render a simple yes-or-no answer to some precise question, a question which has been drawn in as specific a manner as possible.

E. The question is a serious one, but it has been confounded by a discrepancy that exists between the legal and journalistic expectation of what a trial does.

F. It is looked upon as a fact-finding operation, an occasion for the public exposure of all known information regarding a given crime.

Exercise 3

Arrange these sentences into a coherent paragraph that begins with this sentence: *Nobody ever discovered ugliness through photographs.*[7]

A. Even if someone did say that, all it would mean is: "I find that ugly thing . . . beautiful."

B. (The name under which Fox Talbot patented the photograph in 1841 was the calotype: from *kalos*, beautiful.)

C. But many, through photographs, have discovered beauty.

D. Nobody exclaims, "Isn't that ugly! I must take a photograph of it."

E. Except for those situations in which the camera is used to document, or to mark social rites, what moves people to take photographs is finding something beautiful.

Exercise 4

Arrange these sentences into a coherent paragraph.[8]

A. Having, as it sometimes seems, the key to the universe in its very techniques of investigation, science is on a progress of discovery that has no conceivable limit, unless it is the mushroom cloud on the horizon.

B. It is no wonder that we respect the office of scientist, for one mystery after another has yielded to the formidable machinery of scientific method.

C. He is consulted by senators, courted by corporations, and exalted by the popular mind.

D. The scientist is one of the cultural heroes of our age.

E. The triumphs of science seem inexorable as the tide.

F. And with the mysteries, so also numberless human afflictions are closer to our control: hunger and squalor, pain and neurotic anguish, enervating toil and terrifying superstition, perhaps, as Bergson once dared hope, even death itself.

Exercise 5

Revise these thesis statements to ensure they have one central idea/central argument expressed in a specific and precise declarative sentence, confidently worded but not overly detailed.

A. Social networking sites may possibly have caused more harm than good.

B. This paper is about economic recessions.

C. What are the advantages of knowing Latin?

D. This tutorial explains how to register for General Education courses, which can be taken as on-ground courses offered in fall and spring semesters, as well as in the winter intersession and summer session; as online courses offered in fall and spring semesters; and as hybrid courses, offered mostly in spring semester.

E. We should consider the possibility of lowering the unfair and hypocritical national minimum drinking age to 18.

F. Should our college ban alcohol on campus?

G. This report traces the causes of plagiarism and classroom incivility on college campuses.

H. Some action should be taken relative to the use of cell phones in public places.

I. The University should provide more financial aid opportunities and tutoring services to students.

J. I am qualified for your advertised entry-level position in Public Relations because of my education, which includes a soon-to-be-earned bachelor's degree in Public Relations from one of the top schools in the country, where I took courses in PR theory, PR management, and PR writing, as well as courses in persuasion, organizational communication, global communication, crisis management, and social media networking, while earning a 3.95 GPA (the only two B's I got were in GE courses), and because I have completed four internships in public relations—two with PR firms, one in the PR department of a large company, and one with a nonprofit agency; I also worked part-time with a start-up PR firm that gave me two raises in the four months I was there.

Exercise 6

Choose the thesis statement (A, B, C, or D) the other sentences (reasons) support.

1. A. Nell is our top-performing employee.
   B. The company should give Nell a raise.
   C. If we don't reward Nell adequately, she will probably leave for another job.
   D. Nell's work product exceeds her official job duties.

2. **A.** The meal was inexpensive.
    B. The meal was tasty.
    C. The meal was healthy.
    D. The meal was great.

3. **A.** The Wildcats have the best coach in the league.
    B. The Wildcats are experienced in winning.
    C. The Wildcats will win the league championship.
    D. The Wildcats have the best players in the league.

4. **A.** The American Popular Culture course had five exams.
    B. The American Popular Culture course was challenging.
    C. The American Popular Culture course required five papers.
    D. The American Popular Culture course discussed seven books.

5. **A.** The Office of Productivity is managed inefficiently.
    B. The Office of Productivity is overstaffed.
    C. The Office of Productivity is disorganized.
    D. The Office of Productivity offers services that duplicate one another.

Exercise 7

Organizing a clothes closet can help illustrate the skills needed to organize a written message. Both the clothes closet and the written message must be structured into main categories (piles) and subordinate categories (subpiles and beyond) to allow for easy access. Chart how you would organize the ideal clothes closet. Begin by grouping your shirts, pants, sweaters, jackets, and shoes. Then divide each of these main categories into as many subordinate categories as needed. Shirts, for example, could be separated by whether they are dress or casual, followed by sleeve length (long or short), color, and fabric.

Exercise 8

Bring to class a term paper you are working on or have recently completed. Exchange papers with a classmate. Read your classmate's paper and then reverse outline its main ideas/main arguments, subideas/subarguments, and beyond. Discuss whether your message and your classmate's message, as reflected by their reverse outlines, are organized effectively. Are any of the main ideas/main arguments, subideas/subarguments, and beyond out of place? What might be added, deleted, or revised to make the messages more compelling?

Notes

1   Williams, Joseph M. *Style: Toward Clarity and Grace.* University of Chicago Press, 1990, p. 45.

2   Pinker, Steven. *The Sense of Style: The Thinking Person's Guide to Writing in the 21st Century.* Viking, p. 139.

3   Pinker, p. 186.

4   Stewart, James B. *Follow the Story: How to Write Successful Nonfiction.* Simon & Shuster, p. 167.

5   Holmes, Oliver Wendell, Jr. "The Path of the Law." *Harvard Law Review*, vol. 10, no. 8, March 1897, p. 457.

6   Epstein, Edward Jay. *Between Fact and Fiction: The Problem of Journalism.* Vintage, 1975, p. 171.

7   Sontag, Susan. *On Photography.* Farrar, Straus and Giroux, 1977, p. 85.

8   Black, Edwin. *Rhetorical Criticism: A Study in Method.* Macmillan, 1965, p. 1.

Fortifying Sentences, Paragraphs, and Pages

3

This chapter examines additional ways to ensure your sentences, paragraphs, and pages are clear, concise, and compelling. It stresses the importance of developing a unique and relevant point of view, analyzing your audience, and strategizing your message.

Developing a Unique and Relevant Point of View

Your point of view significantly informs your thesis statement, but the two are not identical. More encompassing than your thesis statement, your point of view embodies the myriad values, beliefs, and attitudes reflected in your thesis.

In personal writing, as opposed to formal writing, it is often easier to present a unique and relevant point of view. Most personal writing affords the luxury of selecting the topics you wish to address and then targeting your ideal audience. On whatever subject strikes your fancy, you can offer a uniquely personal point of view aimed at friendly readers wanting to know what you are thinking and doing. Such is not the case in formal writing, where your topics and your audiences are usually assigned, making it more difficult for you to always engage your material. The nature and scope of most workplace writing, for example, is dictated by your professional expertise and position in the company. Similarly, in school you are usually asked to write on specific subjects, according to specific rules, for a specific audience of one: your instructor.

In formal writing, a unique and relevant point of view does not mean simply giving your opinion, let alone without any evidence. Nor does it mean finding and restating an opinion, albeit with evidence, shared by nearly everyone. A *unique* point of view must in some way, no matter how small, be fresh and novel, yet still credible; a *relevant* point of view must be applicable and significant to the reader. Some views will be unique, but not relevant; others will be relevant, but not unique.

A unique and relevant point of view *adds to the conversation* by extending the reader's knowledge and understanding of the subject. The more your writing adds to the conversation, the greater its significance. (This holds true for faculty scholarship as well, although the level of significance required for scholarly publication is much higher.) Settling on topics that do little more than champion the obvious may be safe and easy, but such default choices can divert you from approaching your subject with the kind of passion that drives and sustains your efforts. Choosing the commonplace may also cast you as unoriginal, uninspiring, and lazy.

Even when you write on well-worn topics such as capital punishment, abortion, gun control, marijuana, drug abuse, and euthanasia, your point of view can—and should—still contribute something to the conversation. To merely restate the same standard arguments and evidence that audiences have come to expect on these subjects is to waste your readers' time. Audiences deserve more.

The nature of personal writing offers some clues on how you can distinguish your point of view. In personal writing, you welcome the opportunity to express yourself, to be heard on topics large and small. You impart your views because you want others to appreciate how you see the world. This very mindset should govern your more formal writing as well. If you approach the task of formal writing as yet another opportunity to leave your mark, you are more impelled to produce distinct messages that persuasively resonate with your readers.

Steve Jobs famously said:

Creativity is just connecting things. When you ask creative people how they did something, they feel a little guilty because they didn't really *do* it, they just *saw* something. It seemed obvious to them after a while. That's because they were able to connect experiences they've had and synthesize new things.[1]

Good writers are no different: they push themselves to look beyond the surface, to drill for uncommon connections that will generate a unique and relevant point of view. The willingness to question coupled with the ability to exercise critical thinking skills leads to such discovery. As philosopher and psychologist William James puts it, genius "means little more than the faculty of perceiving in an unhabitual way."[2]

A unique and relevant point of view is more likely to emerge when you are ever mindful of the needs and wants of your audience. Especially when you write formally, you must continually ask yourself: Why would anyone be interested in my message? What makes it significant? Or, more bluntly: Who cares and so what?

The best writers follow what poet Robert Frost would say is the road "less traveled."[3] Granted, you cannot, nor should you, embark on such a trip for every writing assignment. Called upon to primarily report, describe, or explain, you would typically travel a straight and narrow path. But when you are asked to engage in analysis, evaluation, commentary, and critique, the opportunity for exploration avails itself. These tasks invite unique and relevant points of view, the most interesting of which are likely to challenge conventional thinking.

Consider this sample response (Box 3.1) to the following class assignment: Write a personal essay (750 words maximum) on why (or why not) communication leads to a more contented society.

If this essay were to take the form of a longer, more academic paper, (1) what additional evidence would you use to bolster the arguments presented; (2) what other arguments could you make to support the author's position; and (3) how would the paper's writing style and structure differ?

Box 3.1 Overvaluing the Value of Communication

Against the backdrop of an increasingly polarized nation, many of us still cling to the fanciful notion that communication is all-curative. Despite overwhelming evidence to the contrary, we faithfully insist

continued

that if everyone would just communicate more and more openly, the world would surely be a better place. Enhanced by greater understanding and appreciation of one another, the quality of our personal and professional relationships (even those in the political arena), so goes the thinking, would soar because we would come to readily accept each other's point of view.

Yeah, right.

Have we not learned anything from constantly witnessing the dual-sided nature of communication?

Robust dialogue and debate may result in sounder, consensually driven decision-making—assuming, of course, all sides are not intractable and unwilling to compromise. And, yes, encouraging people to communicate gives them the opportunity to express and satisfy their need to be heard. But the *act* of communicating by itself does not magically obviate differences and resolve disputes. Look no further than today's 24-hour barrage of electronic and online political news and commentary: Where precisely is the less divided, less acrimonious climate that increased communication promises?

Nor does the act of communicating function to automatically improve how we perceive and judge each other. If it did, winning over friends and lovers would be so easy: we'd bond more just by talking more. The initial assessment of a first date—*he seems perfect; this could be the one*—would never be upended by the revelations of a second: *He collects Nazi memorabilia? Hitler was actually very misunderstood?*

Everywhere, it seems, the myth of communication as savior is championed and celebrated, but nowhere more prominently than in television and film, whose stories often serve as life lessons for their viewers.

In scripted television, conflict develops and plays out between characters, only to be resolved at show's end by the Great Communication Solution: everyone conveniently explains where he or she is coming from and why, followed by everyone quickly accepting everyone else's explanation. The Great Communication

continued

Solution provides a quick and tidy dramatic solution to any conflict, especially one facing the time constraints of episodic television.

In popular film, the formula is the same. Only rarely does the cinematic experience question the all-curative power of communication. One of the best exceptions is the classic film *Cool Hand Luke*, where the prison warden, Captain (played by Strother Martin), explains to the savvy but incorrigible inmate, Luke Jackson (played by Paul Newman), that his rejection of authority is because he obviously misunderstands prison rules. "What we got here," he says sardonically, "is failure to communicate."

More typical are the scores of romantic comedies that invariably feature the earnest couple facing some issue, usually involving a misunderstanding, which threatens to end their otherwise perfect relationship. Most of the time the "crisis" is so simple that it could be settled by the family dog. Yet here they are, this adorable couple, still deeply in love, about to end it all until, at last, one person finds the courage to apply the Great Communication Solution. A few minutes of conversation later, everything is set straight and the newly enlightened couple are ready to live happily ever after.

In the real world, of course, people don't end marriages simply because someone has misheard or misread the other. And no five-minute dialogue, no matter how poignant, ever permanently stabilized a rocky relationship. True, some relationships end because the couples never learn how to effectively communicate. But many more dissolve or never get started because the participants have communicated all too well and know they want no part of one another.

Communication is a double-edged sword. The more you communicate with anyone, the more you uncover. Some discoveries lead you to like the person more; others cause you to like the person less. For important relationships, honest, in-depth communication is a commitment worth making, but it is still a decision that entails risk. Sometimes you're rewarded; sometimes you're not.

Then again, think of all the people you get along with primarily because you hardly know them. Such relationships survive *because*

continued

they are kept superficial, ensuring that our suspicions of how little we have in common and how differently we see the world are never affirmed. Limiting our communication allows these acquaintances to stay operational. Here and elsewhere it is often our conscious *lack* of communication that continues to save the day.

Analyzing Your Audience

Think Rhetorically

Understanding your audience's values and beliefs allows you to forge a stronger, more rhetorical message. This does not mean speaking out of both sides of your mouth, saying one thing to one audience and the opposite to another. It is not your principles you compromise or adapt. Rather, it is the shaping of your message—how you choose to depict and support your ideas/arguments—that you strategically tailor to your specific audience.

Nowhere is the importance of effective audience analysis and adaptation better illustrated than in the ever common job application letter. Its successful execution demands a level of *rhetorical literacy* that enables you to address your audience's needs and wants. To create this kind of message, you must put yourself in your readers' place by asking: Given what my readers—not me, but *my readers*—need and want, how do I craft an appealing message?

In most application letters, you try to show how your education, skills, and experience would benefit your potential employer. Inexperienced job applicants, however, often make the mistake of stressing the valuable experience *they* would gain if hired. They write sentences like *I would love to work for your company because it would enable me to learn from some of the top professionals in the field as I prepare for a career in . . .* Asking an employer to serve as your personal trainer so you can develop your job skills (and then move on to a better job?) is not exactly adapting to your audience's needs.

Most job application letters, especially from recent college graduates, seem to be a combination of mush and bravado. It is a wonder anyone ever gets hired. First comes the mush. *Ever since I can remember—I think I was maybe 6 or 7 at the time—I've wanted to become an accountant. It's all I ever wanted to do. It's my dream job.* Who isn't passionate about one's career choice when just starting out and eagerly searching for a job? It is not something that separates you from the crowd or provides a compelling reason why you should be hired. More importantly, being passionate does not necessarily mean you are any good.

More mush:

* No one will work harder than I will. [Talk about bold moves to distance yourself from all those other applicants who said they were lethargic.]

* It would be an honor and a privilege to work for an industry-leading company such as yours. [This sort of obsequiousness again makes the strategic error of focusing on how you, not the company, would benefit from your hiring. The implication is that once you have some experience, you will be in a position to move on to another, better job—which is like using *first marriage* to describe one still in progress.]

A good application letter should focus on the reasons and supporting evidence for why the employer would benefit by hiring you.

Employers, for example, often place strong communication skills at the top of their desired job qualifications. Applicants, in turn, usually respond with some variation of *I have very strong communication skills.* Without supporting evidence, this claim means little since no one expects to hear the reverse, *I communicate poorly and always have, but I thought I'd apply anyway.* If you say you communicate well, you need to provide credible, evidence-based support. This can come in the form of work, school, or community-related experiences.

Application letters often proclaim expertise, if not greatness, usually with a string of sentences all starting with *I. I have terrific interpersonal skills. I am an excellent team player. I excel in meeting deadlines. I am better than anyone at multitasking. I am exceptionally conscientious.* The writer is also usually fabulous at withholding any evidence that would support these declarations.

A smarter approach in extolling your virtues while not sounding like a braggart is to let the facts speak for themselves. It is better to write,

I honed my communication skills by working three years in customer service than *I shrewdly added to my already incredible communication skills by devoting myself to working in customer service, where I was awesome.* Ration your adjectives and adverbs when describing your skills and accomplishments.

The test of whether you are making an effective argument in your application letter is twofold: Does your audience perceive your argument to be relevant to your purpose? Does your audience perceive your argument to be supported by sound evidence (sufficient in quality and quantity) and reasoning? An effective argument meets both criteria.

Assume your application letter gives these four reasons why the employer should hire you (your thesis): *I am well trained for the position; I possess strong communication skills; I strive to be a team player; and I want to save the planet.* To win over any prospective employer, these arguments must be seen as germane to why you should be hired. If your reader views your desire to save the planet as irrelevant to job performance, the argument becomes moot and should not be presented, no matter how strong its supporting evidence.

On the other hand, if your prospective employer sees a commitment to saving the planet as central to your job duties, you would want to argue you are so committed, provided you can make the case convincingly. But if your evidence is lacking, you will not persuade your reader, and you may lose credibility. Moreover, the loss of credibility resulting from a poor argument can negatively affect how your audience perceives *all* your arguments. Suddenly, even your well-evidenced ones may be looked upon differently and reevaluated less favorably because you are now seen as less credible. This is particularly true in cases where you argue strongly against something or someone, as in the earlier example that *John should not be elected student body president because he is emotionally unstable.* Were you to make this argument without adequate evidence, it would likely lower your credibility because you would be seen as attacking without sufficient cause. Presenting a badly supported argument is often worse than presenting none at all.

Some writers will knowingly advance a weak argument, hoping it may appeal to someone. They think that a weak argument, at worse, will just be ignored. The larger harm of a weak argument, however, is that it is *not* ignored. Rather, it is processed as a sign of the writer's intelligence and character. It affects the reader's perception of whether the writer is credible and to what extent anything said should be believed.

Whether you are writing an application letter or any other persuasive message, the amount of evidence you provide for your arguments depends on your audience. If readers already agree with you, much less evidence is required than if they are undecided or opposed to your position. Given the brevity of most application letters, why waste time evidencing arguments your audience already accepts? Better yet, why waste time making such arguments? After all, do you really need to convince your prospective employer you want the job, respect the company, and would relish the opportunity to prove yourself?

Play Nice

Sometimes your thoughts need to be qualified, lest you appear simplistic or dogmatic. This type of qualification enhances your credibility because it portrays you as thoughtful and reasonable. Other times, writers will say, *I think . . . , I believe . . . ,* or *I feel . . .* when it is obvious from the text they are offering their opinion. This is more of a rhetorical nicety, an acknowledgment meant to suggest that the writer is not issuing pronouncements but, instead, presenting a viewpoint with which others may disagree.

Some contend that the use of *I* helps beginning writers articulate their message insofar as it leads them to assume greater ownership of their ideas/arguments. Still, experienced writers limit their use of *I*, especially in formal writing where its overuse can cast you as self-centered and overbearing. Although *I* is preferable to speaking in third person (*this writer*) or resorting to the imperial we (*we found*), *I* draws attention to the writer and away from the text. Overuse of *I* can undermine the credibility of reports, proposals, research papers, and other documents that must typify objectivity.

Some writers overqualify their ideas in hopes of achieving greater precision. Many more do so to protect themselves, believing that qualification will somehow insulate them against future criticism and blame. *I never said we should do it; I said it was something we could potentially consider doing or not doing.* Resist the temptation to seek refuge behind a wall of *apparently, appears, approximately, generally, may, maybe, might, perhaps, possibly, seems,* and *usually.* From the ultracautious comes the multiple hedge. *It appears perhaps it may be possible for me to limit my use of qualifying words.* Four qualifying words—*appears, perhaps, may,* and *possible*—in a single sentence? Any one word would suffice. Writers who overqualify come across as timid and uncommitted.

Some writers go in the opposite direction. Desperately wanting to sound confident, they overstate their case and become insufferable. Their tone is that of the know-it-all. *My many years of executive experience and my numerous leadership awards received over the past two decades allow me to expertly assess your situation and to tell you where you have made some naive mistakes that I am happy to correct because I feel an obligation to . . . yada, yada, yada.* And how many times have we seen stunts like these:

- Any intelligent, rational person can see that my position is correct. [Right, only an idiot would disagree with you. Nice try.]

- Any idiot can see that my position is correct. [Now I'm an idiot because I agree with you? Okay, then, I disagree with you.]

Quality ideas/arguments do not require prefacing that tells the audience just how good they are. You do not need to add: *A magnificent and extremely persuasive example that supports my case . . .* , *another terrific reason why I believe . . .* , *a great point that beautifully illustrates what I have been saying . . .* Solid ideas/arguments can stand on their own merits; they don't need applause signs.

It is also unnecessary to negatively annotate the other side's ideas/ arguments, however woeful. State and refute the idea/argument without engaging in this sort of battering: *My opponent has come to the silly and ridiculous conclusion that most Picasso paintings are overpriced because . . .* A single, carefully chosen word can be far more suggestive. *Curiously, my opponent has concluded that most Picasso paintings are overpriced given how much the artist spent for the canvas and paint.*

Part of being fair and gracious is accepting that intent and function are not the same. The effect of one's words or actions do not necessarily prove a congruent intent. When people misfire, it is seldom because they try to fail. Assigning evil motives to your subjects solely because their words or actions went awry is unreasonable and unfair. In the absence of knowing your subject's intent, it is best to keep your message centered on what you do know for sure.

Prudent writers, moreover, refrain from distorting information to build their case. Adapting penny-wise and pound-foolish tactics, many writers mischaracterize the views of others. Their frequent use of the *straw man* argument (also known as the straw man fallacy) serves as a good example. The straw man argument is a fabrication that distorts your opponent's position to make it easier to refute. Like a straw man, the mischaracterization is a flimsy fake you can pick apart.

Your opponent says, for example, that consenting adults should be allowed to view adult pornography in the privacy of their homes. The straw man characterization: *The other side would like to legalize pornography so children can stare at naked adults all day long.* In other words, your opponent is a dangerous extremist who cannot be trusted.

Or your opponent maintains that pornography needs to be more regulated to protect young children. The straw man characterization: *The other side, which obviously does not believe in the First Amendment and never has, wants to control our personal lives and dictate everything we can and cannot watch.* In other words, your opponent is a dangerous extremist who cannot be trusted.

Straw man arguments ultimately impugn your credibility. A better, nobler approach is to practice the opposite: describe the other side's position so accurately that any of its proponents would agree with your portrayal. Then refute the position with strong, principled arguments. Treating the views of others with this kind of respect and dignity raises your credibility and potential to be compelling.

Recognize That, Yes, Women Do Exist

Nearly as offensive as the straw man argument, gender-specific pronouns (*he* or *she; him* or *her; his* or *hers*) alienate many readers, who view such pronouns as stereotypical. In response, many companies, organizations, and publications have adopted policies against the use of sexist pronouns, which are seen as insensitive and outdated. Fortunately, you can easily change gender-specific pronouns.

The three best options are to replace the sexist pronoun with another word, restructure the sentence to eliminate the pronoun, or pluralize the sentence's subject or object so it requires a plural pronoun.

Replace the pronoun.

ORIGINAL   The University required the faculty member to complete **his** travel request before attending the conference on Writing Renovation.

REVISION   The University required the faculty member to complete a travel request before attending the conference on Writing Renovation.

ORIGINAL   **His** company's budget limited technical writers to 95-word instructional manuals.

REVISION   The company's budget limited technical writers to 95-word instructional manuals.

Restructure the sentence.

ORIGINAL   If a Chief Financial Officer is loved, **he** is never forgotten.

REVISION   A Chief Financial Officer who is loved is never forgotten.

ORIGINAL   Any IT consultant should be computer literate if **he** expects to be hired.

REVISION   Any IT consultant expecting to be hired should be computer literate.

Pluralize the subject or object.

ORIGINAL   A student cannot graduate unless **he** passes the Graduate Writing Test.

REVISED   Students cannot graduate unless they pass the Graduate Writing Test.

ORIGINAL   Professor Kuhl required each student to submit **his** paper in digital format.

REVISED   Professor Kuhl required all students to submit their papers in digital format.

Other options:

- **Combine male and female pronouns.** Sometimes only *he or she*, *he/she*, *his or her*, or *his/her* will do. A bit wordy, this option is best used sparingly. S/he is better, but it never quite caught on.

- **Alternate gender-specific pronouns.** Use the male pronoun for one example and the female pronoun for another, or, as found in some children's books, use male pronouns in one chapter and female pronouns in the next. Alternating gender-specific pronouns, however, can be disorienting for some readers.

- **Ignore the grammatical rule.** A grammatically incorrect but increasingly popular solution, even with a growing number of linguists (but not endorsed here), is to go ahead and use plural pronouns when their referent nouns are singular. *If a Chief Financial Officer is loved, they are never forgotten.*

Strategizing Your Case

The nature of your content invites certain strategic choices and organizational patterns over others. Making the best decisions depends on knowing what your thesis statement entails and what you must prove to gain its acceptance.

From the discipline of Communication Studies come useful lessons on how to categorize and organize messages strategically. Courses in public speaking and argumentation have long conceptualized informative and persuasive speeches in ways that can be adapted and generalized to most informative and persuasive written messages. Just as the speaker's purpose invites certain organizational patterns and strategic choices, so, too, does the writer's thesis.

The categories delineated below serve as a guide, not as a template, for constructing informative and persuasive written messages. They may require additional adaptation depending on the specific requirements of various writing assignments.

The demands of informative versus persuasive messages can be more easily understood by first considering the nature and characteristics of persuasive messages.

Strategize Persuasive Messages

Before you write any persuasive message, determine whether you are advocating a proposition of fact, value, or policy.

A **fact proposition** (thesis) proposes that something was/was not, is/is not, or will/will not be true. It does not make any value judgment about the truth, nor does it recommend any course of action in light of it. When you argue a fact proposition, you ask your audience to accept or reject a "larger" factual conclusion based on your presentation of "smaller" supporting facts. Universally agreed-upon facts—for example, the sun rises in the east and sets in the west, George Washington was the first president of the United States, or Maine is north of Florida—do not qualify for debate. Arguable fact propositions on which we disagree are another matter. *The dinosaurs were killed by a meteor shower. Toxins cause Parkinson's disease. The Consumer Price Index will decrease next year.*

Fact propositions dominate criminal courtroom proceedings. The prosecution, for example, claims that Neumann committed the murder (big fact), as evidenced by several smaller facts: he threatened several times to kill the victim, he was seen arguing with the victim just before gunshots were heard, he fled the country immediately after the crime, gunpowder residue was found on his hands, his fingerprints were on the gun that killed the victim, his clothes were splattered with the victim's blood, an eyewitness saw him shoot the victim, and he bragged on his Facebook page about killing the victim.

Most fact propositions can be organized in one of two ways.

1. When you argue that something is true because it meets the criteria, or exhibits the qualities, that define it as true, you are using a **definitional criteria design**. Take this example: *Many first-year college students lack essential writing skills.* In supporting this thesis, you must explicitly or implicitly define what you mean by "essential writing skills." Often your arguments will implicitly reference your defining criteria. Note the implicit criterion (italicized) that forms part of each main argument in these sentences:

I.   Many first-year college students do not know *how to choose a thesis.*

II. Many first-year college students do not know *how to organize ideas and arguments.*

III. Many first-year college students do not know *how to write grammatically correct sentences.*

Irrespective of how well you were to develop these arguments, your readers would not be persuaded if they did not already accept your implicit definitional criteria (choosing a thesis, organizing ideas/arguments, and knowing grammar constitute or define *essential writing skills*). You might, then, first need to explicitly state and justify your definitional criteria. Following your essay's introduction, for example, your second paragraph might begin: *Essential writing skills include knowing how to choose a thesis, organize ideas and arguments, and write grammatically correct sentences.* After establishing the validity of these criteria, you would show why first-year students do not meet the standard.

2. When you argue that one fact causes another fact, you are using a **causal design**. If you were to contend that the *lack of essential writing skills leads to lower grades*, you would be maintaining that the existence of one fact, lack of essential writing skills, causes another fact, lower grades. This proposition/thesis does not require you to show that students *do* lack essential writing skills; you need only prove that the absence of those skills would cause lower grades. The body of your message might develop these arguments:

I.   Lack of essential writing skills diminishes the professor's understanding of what you are saying.

II. Lack of essential writing skills diminishes the professor's perception of your knowledge.

III. Lack of essential writing skills diminishes the professor's perception of your intelligence.

A causal design differs from the narrower *causal argument*. Messages organized around a causal design have as their purpose to establish an overall causal relationship, which is reflected in the thesis statement (*Lack of essential writing skills leads to lower grades*) and supported with causal arguments. Causal arguments can also be used to develop propositions of value and policy.

Creating well-reasoned, well-evidenced causal arguments precludes your readers from raising damaging counter-arguments to your position. Your analysis should always take into account these possibilities: Is there a direct causal relationship (cause = effect; effect = cause)? Is there another, more likely cause (of the effect) than the cause you give? Do multiple causes, in addition to those you present, collectively produce the causal relationship? Does the cause (or causes) lead to other effects for which you have not accounted?

A **value proposition** (thesis) proposes the assigning of a specific value to an agreed-upon fact. It does not propose any course of action relating to the value, although, as earlier discussed, values and beliefs ultimately affect attitudes and behaviors. The value judgment expressed in a value proposition is one of right/wrong, ethical/unethical, good/bad, or fair/unfair about something whose past, present, or future existence is not at issue. _Killing animals for food_ [agreed-upon fact] _is immoral. It was unfair to _award_ _every student an A in the course regardless of his/her performance_ [agreed-upon fact]. _To stereotype Muslims_ [agreed-upon fact] _is wrong._ A value proposition can also comparatively evaluate, asserting that something is better, superior, nobler—or in some other way more worthy or less worthy—than something else.

Value judgments derive from **valuational criteria**. Similar to definitional criteria, valuational criteria can be explicitly or implicitly referenced. And similar to definitional criteria, they are implicitly referenced when they are likely to already be accepted by your audience as a valid standard for your judgment. For example, if you were to propose, _The bank's loan modification program_ [agreed-upon fact] _was unethical,_ and then proceed to argue, (1) _The bank discriminated against minority customers_; (2) _The bank deceived customers_; and (3) _The bank forged documents,_ you would be referencing your implicit evaluation criteria—discrimination, deception, and forgery constitute acting unethically—in your arguments. You would not need to explicitly establish the validity of these criteria, given their near-universal acceptance. Instead, you would focus on proving the bank committed the unethical acts.

On the other hand, when valuational criteria are subject to dispute, they need to be explicitly defended, as in this thesis: _Dogs are superior to cats._ The agreed-upon facts are that dogs and cats exist. Should a value proposition contain disputed words or terms, advocacy cannot go forward until the disputes are resolved. For example, if you were to argue that dogs are superior to extraterrestrials, you would need to suspend the (value) debate until first settling a fact proposition: _Extraterrestrials exist._

In proposing that dogs are superior to cats, you could offer these arguments:

I.   Dogs are smarter than cats.

II. Dogs are more loyal than cats.

III. Dogs are more affectionate than cats.

IV. Dogs are more protective than cats.

Should your audience just happen to include several cat lovers, you would first need to convince them that intelligence, loyalty, affection, and protection are valid criteria for determining a superior pet, or, more precisely, that these qualities should be valued over other qualities. Cat lovers could counter that your criteria are not valid or that they are incomplete because they do not include such traits as independence and self-sufficiency; nor do your criteria take into account that cats catch mice, groom themselves, and do not bark. Because cat lovers are unlikely to fully accept the validity of your criteria, convincing them that dogs are superior to cats will prove elusive no matter how strong your evidence that dogs are more intelligent, loyal, affectionate, and protective.

If your readers were to accept your criteria of what constitutes a superior pet, you would still need to show that dogs meet the criteria better than cats. One could contend that cats, not dogs, are smarter, more loyal, more affectionate, and more protective; or cats are smarter than dogs, and this quality alone outweighs the other three. Your readers could also integrate a portion of your criteria with a larger portion of their own criteria and argue that cats are superior to dogs because they are smarter, more independent, and more self-sufficient. All of which in the end suggests it is probably best to own both a dog and a cat.

A **policy proposition** (thesis) proposes that an existing policy should be changed or abolished or that some new policy should be adopted where there was none. A policy proposition may also argue that a policy should *not* be adopted. "Policy" broadly refers to the current state of affairs or how things operate now, which is called the *status quo*. An affirmatively worded policy proposition (one without the word "not" in it) proposes an action that would alter the status quo. Policy propositions usually contain the word *should*. *The federal minimum wage should be raised to $15 an hour. Cell phone use should be prohibited in public places. The terminally ill should be allowed to end their lives.*

One typical way to organize a policy proposition is by following a **problem–solution design**. You present the significant problem(s) with the status quo and then provide a solution. Frequently, the wording of your policy proposition will reference your solution. For example, your solution to the problem caused by the current minimum federal wage is to raise it to $15; your solution to the problem of cell phone use in public places is to prohibit that use; your solution to the problem of the terminally ill having to suffer is to allow them to end their lives. In a problem–solution design, you establish the problem and then return, if necessary, to detail your solution.

The problem–solution design can be illustrated by an example similar to *John should not be elected student body president.* If you were to say, *John should be fired as company CEO,* the proposition, which references the solution (firing John), could similarly be supported by showing that he *is dishonest, cannot manage,* and *is emotionally unstable*—three arguments that speak to the problem of his serving as company CEO (the status quo).

When you advocate a major change in policy, such as *John should be fired as company CEO,* you must prove that a problem exists and that it is *significant* enough to warrant the time, effort, and risk involved in making a major policy change. Proposing a major change to solve a minor problem is neither cost-effective nor responsible. We know this intuitively. It is the reason why when your otherwise perfectly running car needs new brakes, you spring for the repair; you don't fix the problem by buying a new car. But should the needed repair exceed the car's value, the repair now becomes a significant problem usually best resolved by a major change (i.e., finding another car).

The act of firing John is not a complicated solution requiring detailed discussion of its execution; you need only remind your reader, usually at or near the end of your paper, that firing John would end his flawed leadership of the company. In other cases, however, the solution and its implementation may require more discussion and justification, which would typically come after you have addressed the need for change (the problem).

Your analysis of your proposition/thesis, especially your assessment of the degree to which your audience initially favors/disfavors your position, guides you in deciding how much time and effort to devote to establishing the problem and explaining your solution. The importance of the latter cannot be overstated. No matter how effective your indictment of the status quo, your message will be lacking if it skirts the detailed solution your specific proposal may require, or, worse, it presents a dubious solution, leaving readers to conclude:

- Yes, I agree that illegal drug trafficking is a significant problem, but shooting drug users on the spot is not the best answer.

- Yes, homelessness is a significant problem, but shipping the homeless to Antarctica is absurd.

- Yes, the football team's record is a significant problem, but abolishing the program goes too far.

Indeed, it is common for audiences to agree that a problem exists but to disagree on how to rectify it.

To illustrate how a solution is developed, consider this proposition: *The University should adopt a more proactive policy for reducing student cheating.* First, you would have to establish that campus cheating is a serious problem. You might argue that cheating is rampant, worsening, and being ignored by school administrators. (These arguments would be introduced by topic sentences heading the sections that develop the arguments.) Or, you could just briefly summarize the arguments if you knew for sure your audience would agree on the problem. Second, your solution would need to satisfy these concerns: What do I mean by a *more proactive policy*? How would the new policy reduce cheating? Would it be practical? What would be the ramifications of its adoption? One possible solution, though certainly unconventional, would have these planks:

I. The University can reduce cheating by paying "student spotters" to report on other students who cheat. The program would be set up like this . . .

II. Using "student spotters" will lead to more reported instances of cheating because students are in the best position to know what other students are doing. Students live together, eat together, and study together.

III. Many students will stop cheating once they realize they have a greater chance of getting caught. This has been shown by . . .

IV. The cost of this program, including paying students and setting up an on-campus Cheating Detection Office with a full-time director, would be $500,000 a year, which could be raised by adding a $25 annual "anti-cheating fee" to the student activity fee.

V. Although many naysayers would have you believe that students reporting on other students is an awful idea that would lead to a hostile, police-state environment, this is not true. First, the reporting process would be anonymous . . .

When your audience already agrees with you about what is wrong with the status quo, it is usually unnecessary—political oratory being a notable exception—to spend significant time arguing that the problem exists. The better strategy is to underscore how your proposed solution provides the ideal remedy. For example, assume John—the CEO, not the student body president—gets fired, thanks to your well-articulated report outlining his faults. The company then announces it is looking for a new CEO who can restore honesty, managerial competence, and emotional stability to its top leadership post. These job qualifications reflect what is now missing from the company (the problem), which it hopes to correct by hiring a new CEO (the solution).

In presenting your case for who should lead the company, you would not have to address why the company should hire an honest, managerially competent, emotionally stable leader; on this, everyone agrees. Rather, you would want to concentrate on why your proposed candidate, Neal, would solve the problem.

After an introductory paragraph that includes your thesis statement, *Neal should be appointed CEO*, your reasons could be introduced with topic sentences like these:

I.   Neal would be an honest CEO.

II. Equally important, Neal would effectively manage the company.

III. Furthermore, Neal would bring emotional stability to the position.

For these reasons, Neal's hiring would solve the company's needs (the problem).

A variation of the problem–solution design is the **problem–cause–solution design**. *John should be fired as company CEO* (because)

I.   The company has suffered declining revenues. (problem)

II. The company has suffered declining profits. (problem)

III. The company is continually being sued by public and private entities. (problem)

IV. John's leadership has caused these problems. (cause)

V. Firing John as CEO would solve these problems. (solution)

Sometimes you may want to persuade your audience that the status quo should be changed not so much because a clear-cut problem exists, but because change would be advantageous. In a **comparative advantages design**, you show how your proposed change would be comparatively and significantly advantageous over the status quo. For example, a friend tries to convince you to move to another apartment. She proposes that living in the new apartment would be comparatively advantageous to staying in your current one because the new place is bigger, nicer, pet friendly, and cheaper. Each advantage would be worded as an argument and introduced with a topic sentence.

I. Moving to the new apartment would give you more space.

II. This space would also be more luxurious.

III. Freddy would benefit from the larger dog run in the new apartment.

IV. Best of all, rent for the new apartment is much less than what you now pay.

If you were to point out that these advantages identify needs not being met by the status quo and reflect an implicit problem with the status quo, you would be correct. In a comparative–advantages design as opposed to a problem–solution design, however, the structure of your arguments focuses on comparing the proposed change to the status quo and showing how and why the change would bring about significant advantages over the status quo.

Renovation Tip

Working on the easier sections of your paper before tackling the harder parts can boost your confidence and creative momentum. You are also less likely to become discouraged if you take on the more challenging sections *after* completing a substantial portion of your paper.

Strategize Informative Messages

When you present an informative message, you assume the role of teacher rather than advocate. Your primary intent is to inform your readers by describing or explaining something about which they have limited knowledge; it is not to persuade them to accept a larger (debatable) truth, embrace a value, or take an action. Such may occur, but it is not your objective.

An informative message may seem similar to a fact proposition. The key difference is that a fact proposition advances a partisan position on a debatable, usually controversial, question of past, present, or future fact. *What killed the dinosaurs? Do toxins cause Parkinson's disease? Will the Consumer Price Index increase next year?* An informative message answers a different kind of factual question, one that asks for a neutral presentation of generally accepted information. *What types of dinosaurs existed? What are the symptoms of Parkinson's disease? How does one measure the Consumer Price Index?*

Writers sometimes mischaracterize persuasive messages as informative. Using words associated with informative communication, they present persuasive propositions under the guise of informing their readers. *This paper will describe how the earth was first populated by Martians* (fact proposition). *I will discuss why cheating at solitaire is wrong* (value proposition). *Here is an explanation of why the Theatre Department's online acting courses should be dropped from the curriculum* (policy proposition). It is misleading to label your thesis as informative when your intent is to persuade.

Writing an informative message is not necessarily easier than drafting a persuasive one. Each presents a different set of challenges. In a persuasive message, you try to move readers toward your position by presenting audience-appealing arguments. In an informative message, you seek to enlighten your audience by presenting relevant and interesting information. Unlike persuasive texts whose subject matter often commands attention, informative texts examine topics that sometimes have a tougher time drawing and sustaining reader interest. On the other hand, informative messages usually do not meet the attitudinal resistance faced by many persuasive messages.

Informative messages can be organized in various ways, but the most common designs include **categorical** (or **topical**), **categorical comparative**, **causal**, **chronological/sequential**, and **narrative**.

Categorical (or Topical) Design. A categorical design breaks a topic into categories. If you were describing a play, for example, you could sketch its character(s), setting, conflict, and resolution. Heading the first paragraph of each category would be a topic sentence that summarizes the discussion to follow. (The example of how to organize baseball equipment in Chapter 2, Box 2.6 exemplifies a categorical design.)

Categorical–Comparative Design. A categorical–comparative design compares two or more items for the purpose of enlightening each. This design works best for a comparative analysis, a message type popular in business and academia that features description, interpretation, and evaluation. A mistake writers commonly make when comparing items is to discuss each item separately across all categories, one item at a time. In effect, the items become the main headings, replacing the more important categories for comparison, which are downgraded to subheadings. This structure makes it difficult to process comparisons because they are not made side-by-side, category-by-category.

Box 3.2 shows how *not* to organize a comparative analysis of three companies. In the example, readers are expected to remember how Company 1 performed across five categories as they read about Company 2. Then, they must recall how Companies 1 and 2 compared as they learn about Company 3. Too much is asked of the reader.

A categorical–comparative design that features a linear, side-by-side comparison of items (shown in Box 3.3) allows for quicker processing and easier remembering of their similarities and differences. It offers a more integrated way to organize this kind of message because readers can immediately see how the items compare across each category, one category at a time.

Causal Design. As noted in the discussion of causal propositions of fact, your message will follow a causal design when your overall purpose is to establish a causal relationship. Each of your main ideas may reflect a "stand-alone" causal relationship that directly supports your thesis. Or your main ideas may establish a causal relationship by building upon one another in support of your thesis. Examples of each approach:

Box 3.2

COMPANY 1 [heading]

Mission Statement [subheading]

Products and Services

Company Sites

Revenue and Income

Employee Training and Development

COMPANY 2 [heading]

Mission Statement [subheading]

Products and Services

Company Sites

Revenue and Income

Employee Training and Development

COMPANY 3 [heading]

Mission Statement [subheading]

Products and Services

Company Sites

Revenue and Income

Employee Training and Development

Box 3.3

Mission Statement [heading]

[comparison of companies 1, 2, and 3; depending on the length of the comparison, it may be helpful to include subheadings in the form of the three company names]

_____
_____
_____

Products and Services

[comparison of companies 1, 2, and 3]

_____
_____
_____
_____

Company Sites

[comparison of companies 1, 2, and 3]

_____
_____
_____

Revenues and Income

[comparison of companies 1, 2, and 3]

_____
_____
_____

Employee Training and Development

[comparison of companies 1, 2, and 3]

_____
_____
_____
_____

Thesis statement: Various natural and man-made events can cause an earthquake.

I. A ruptured geological fault can cause an earthquake.

II. A volcanic eruption can cause an earthquake.

III. A landslide can cause an earthquake.

IV. A nuclear explosion can cause an earthquake.

Thesis statement: The earthquake raised the cost of housing.

I. The earthquake destroyed many homes and apartments.

II. Thousands of stranded homeowners and apartment dwellers needed new housing.

III. The resulting shortage of available homes and apartments drove up prices.

Chronological/Sequential Design. A chronological design orders the elements of your message based on time. The chronology can start at any time and weave forth and back, but it will usually go from past to present or from present to past. When you give historical context to your subject and trace its temporal development, for example, you are using a chronological design. If you were writing a paper on how the NCAA Basketball Tournament evolved into a 64-team contest, you could organize the body of your message along the lines of these topic sentences:

I. The first NCAA Basketball Tournament, played in 1939, included eight teams.

II. In 1951, twice as many teams, 16, were invited to the tournament.

III. The tournament doubled to 32 teams in 1975.

IV. Within a six-year period, 1979–1985, the number of participating schools increased four more times, reaching its present number of 64 teams in 1985.

V. Today, some have proposed increasing the tournament to 96 teams, with the top 32 teams having a first-round bye.

Similar to a chronological design, a sequential design is time-based in the sense it describes a step-by-step process or task. (The popular how-to message often uses a sequential design, where each step of the how-to process or task becomes a main idea.) If you were to explain how to report a car accident, your main ideas might read:

I.   Determine if you, the other driver, any passengers, or any pedestrians are injured or may be injured.

II. Call 911 to request medical help, if necessary, and to possibly request police assistance.

III. Once help is on its way, exchange insurance information with the other driver.

IV. Be sure to notify your insurance company within 24 hours of the accident.

Narrative Design. A narrative design allows you to present your message in the form of a story. Although a narrative design does not have summarizing topic sentences, most readers have little trouble picking out the story's main ideas. In a *New Yorker* article chronicling the lives of those who have committed suicide by jumping off San Francisco's Golden Gate Bridge, Tad Friend's narrative includes this poignant passage:

> On December 17, 2001, fourteen-year-old Marissa Imrie, a petite and attractive straight-A student who had planned to become a psychiatrist, left her second-period class at Santa Rosa High School, took a hundred-and-fifty-dollar taxi ride to the Golden Gate, and jumped to her death. Though Marissa was always very hard on herself and had lately complained of severe headaches and insomnia, her mother, Renee Milligan, had no inkling of her plans. "She called us 'the glue girls,' we were so close," Milligan told me. "She'd never spoken about the bridge, and we'd never even visited it."
>
> When Milligan examined her daughter's computer afterward, she discovered that Marissa had been visiting a how-to Web site about suicide that featured grisly autopsy photos. The site notes that many suicide methods are ineffective (poison is fatal only fifteen per cent of the time, drug overdose twelve per cent, and wrist cutting

a mere five per cent) and therefore recommends bridges, noting that "jumps from higher than . . . 250 feet over water are almost always fatal." Milligan bought the proprietor of the site's book, "Suicide and Attempted Suicide," and read the following sentence: "The Golden Gate Bridge is to suicides what Niagara Falls is to honeymooners." She returned the book and gave the computer away.

Every year, Marissa had written her mother a Christmas letter reflecting on the year's events. On Christmas Day that year, Milligan, going through her daughter's things, found her suicide note. It was tucked into "The Chronicles of Narnia," which sat beside a copy of "Seven Habits of Highly Effective Teenagers." The note ended with a plea: "Please forgive me. Don't shut your-selves off from the world. Everyone is better off without this fat, disgusting, boring girl. Move on."

Renee Milligan could not. "When I went to my optometrist, I realized he has big pictures of the Golden Gate in his office, and I had to walk out," she said. "The image of the bridge is everywhere. San Francisco *is* the Golden Gate Bridge—I can't escape it."[4]

Friend's narrative functions every bit as powerfully as would a thesis-driven, topic sentence style to illustrate the lessons revealed by this tragedy: young teenagers are not immune from depression. Spurred by negative, distorted perceptions of self-worth, they suffer alone, their pain unnoticed or unaddressed until it is too late. And for the family they leave behind, the mourning never quite ends.

A message can combine different designs, leading to a variety of organizational possibilities. A categorical or categorical–comparative design can include a narrative that functions as a summary; a narrative can be told chronologically; a chronology can historically trace an evolving causal relationship; and so forth. Although these designs lend themselves to informative messages, they can be imported to persuasive messages as well. Whatever design you choose should be appropriate to your specific content and facilitate your building of a unified, coherent message.

EXERCISES

Exercise 1

Think of a topic about which you have significant knowledge. What would be an example of a fresh, informative, or persuasive thesis you would find unique and relevant?

Exercise 2

Write an application letter for an ideal entry-level job position to which you aspire. Summarize your education, training, experience, and accomplishments using a verb-oriented style that minimally employs adjectives, adverbs, and the word *I*.

Exercise 3

Identify the following propositions as either fact, value, or policy.

A. All public high schools should enroll only same-sex students.

B. Reality TV shows instill a negative view of society.

C. Technology has caused more harm than good.

D. Public colleges should be free for all citizens of the United States.

E. The killing of any animal for clothing should be prohibited.

F. Rap music is hate speech.

G. People who have a college degree are smarter than those who do not.

H. Attending college is a waste of time.

I. All executions should be televised.

J. Downloading music or films for personal use is unethical.

K. Bullfighting is inhumane.

L. The United States Food and Drug Administration should outlaw all processed foods.

M. Money is the root of all pleasure.

N. Employers should not be allowed to discriminate against people having tattoos and piercings.

O. Zombies exist.

Notes

1   Jobs, Steve. Quoted in Gary Wolfe, "Steve Jobs: The Next Insanely Great Thing." *Wired Magazine*, Feb. 1, 1996, www.wired.com/1996/02/jobs-2/

2   James, William. *The Principles of Psychology*. Vol. 2, Henry Holt, 1890, p. 110. 2 vols.

3   Frost, Robert. "The Road Not Taken." *Mountain Interval*. Henry Holt, 1916, p. 9.

4   Friend, Tad. "Jumpers: The Fatal Grandeur of the Golden Gate Bridge." *New Yorker*, Nov. 13, 2003, www.newyorker.com/magazine/2003/10/13/jumpers. Reprinted by permission of International Creative Management, Inc. Copyright © 2003 by Tad Friend.

4

Adding the Finishing Touches

Driving Home Your Message Visually

Effective formatting visually reinforces your thesis and supporting ideas/arguments. And it makes your message more inviting and easier to process, serving as yet another tool for reducing miscommunication.

Presented with an unparagraphed block of single-spaced type devoid of any variation in layout or a text organized into several paragraphs with headings and subheadings, which would you choose to read? Some forms, such as academic and journalistic writing, follow more conservative formatting, notably in their use of bullets, italics, and boldface. You must know your audience and adapt accordingly.

Many academic style guides, such as the *Publication Manual of the American Psychological Association* (APA) and *The Chicago Manual of Style* (CMS), give specific directions for formatting headings and subheadings. (*MLA Handbook* [MLA] is less prescriptive.) In addition, many companies, institutions, and government entities have their own formatting requirements. Templates that ensure consistency and professionalism are incorporated into the organization's word-processing programs. What is often missing from many of these guidelines, however, is any rationale for why they make sense from a visual communication perspective.

When you are not obligated to follow prescribed formatting guidelines, you can pick from an array of memo, letter, e-mail, and report formats one that best meets your needs and tastes. Your formatting should be consistent, logical, and attractive.

You never want to do this:

To: All employees of LuC Press
FROM: Josie Mahoney
Date: August 17, 2016
SUBJECT: RK Gunning Business Writing Workshop

FROM and SUBJECT are in all upper case letters (all capitals), but To and Date are not; entries are double spaced, except between **FROM** and Date; and only **FROM** is boldfaced. Such inconsistencies signify a writer who has no attention to detail. Now consider this version:

TO: All employees of LuC Press
FROM: Josie Mahoney
DATE: August 17, 2016
SUBJECT: RK Gunning Business Writing Workshop

Consistent fonts, equal spacing, and vertically aligned entries make this version easier to read.

Rely on Headings and Subheadings

To avoid confusion about what your headings and subheadings summarize, visually position them closer to what they head than to what they follow. When headings "float"—equally distanced between the texts they follow and the texts they precede—it can be difficult to make quick sense as to which headings and texts go together, especially when your paper includes multiple levels of headings.

If you were formatting the body of *John should not be elected student body president*, a double-spaced manuscript with indented paragraphs should look something like the sample text in Box 4.1.

In addition to the main headings and subheadings being aligned with the texts they overview, the sample's formatting enhances message readability and appeal in several ways.

1. The main headings and subheadings clearly and concisely summarize the writer's viewpoint. They are not simply topics, such as *honesty,*

Box 4.1

Lacks Honesty

Foremost, John should not be elected student body president because he is dishonest. This dishonesty takes several forms.

He Lies

_____

_____

_____

He Cheats

_____

_____

_____

He Steals

_____

_____

_____

Lacks Management Skills

_____

_____

_____

Lacks Emotional Stability

_____

_____

_____

management skills, and *emotional stability,* which would give readers little direction or heads-up about the arguments to follow. In a persuasive message, your headings and subheadings should be abstracted versions of your main arguments and subarguments; they should express your viewpoint.

2. The main headings are linguistically parallel to one another, as are the subheadings. *He lies, He cheats, He steals* share a parallel structure: each begins with the subject *He,* followed by an intransitive verb. The subheadings would not have been parallel had *He lies* been followed by *He has a problem with cheating* and *Stealing is like a hobby to him.* Wording your headings in parallel language, when possible, emphasizes how your ideas/arguments interrelate and how they collectively address the larger idea/argument to which they are subordinate.

3. The main headings are visually consistent with one another, as are the subheadings, in terms of font (font = typeface, typeface style, and point size). Main headings and subheadings are bolded, with the first letter of each word capitalized. The main headings are in larger point size than the subheadings, although another option would be to set the main headings in all capitals. All capitals, however, can be difficult to read in extended form and can come across as if you are shouting at your reader; their use should be restricted to the shortest of copy (such as headings).

4. The subheadings (*He lies, He cheats, He steals*) are visually subordinate to the superior main heading (*Lacks Honesty*). Headings are visually subordinate when they are presented in lower versus upper case, set in smaller versus larger point size, styled regularly versus boldly, left justified versus page centered, or placed in-text versus above-text. Formatting that visually distinguishes superior headings from subordinate headings drives home the structure of your message.

   If the subheadings in the example had included sub-subheadings (third-level headings), they, too, would have had to be visually subordinate. For instance, if John were guilty of two types of lying— fabricating facts and excluding facts—both sub-subarguments could have been introduced with *in-text* headings. Positioning a heading *in* the text rather than *above* the text reduces the heading's visual prominence because it no longer stands alone. Instead, it becomes part of the text, as shown in Box 4.2.

Box 4.2

Lacks Honesty

Foremost, John should be fired because he is dishonest. This dishonesty takes several forms.

He Lies

Fabricates facts. _____

_____

_____

Excludes facts. _____

_____

_____

5. Beyond providing emphasis, the bolding of the sample's main and subordinate headings helps separate them from their accompanying texts. When headings and subheadings bleed into their texts because they are aligned too closely without sufficient visual separation, they impair readability. In particular, in-text headings, which trail their texts more closely, must be clearly contrasted.

Renovation Tip

Single-spaced text, which is harder to read than double-spaced text, is better suited for shorter messages. In a single-spaced document, you can choose either *block* style, where the entire text is left justified, or *semi-block* style, where each paragraph is indented; in both styles, you double space between paragraphs. Again, main and subordinate headings must be visually attached to their respective texts.

Befriend Bullets and Numbers

Bullets draw attention to selected elements of your message. Once the computer replaced the typewriter, bullets became an available option in various forms, such as dots, open circles, boxes and shadowed boxes, and check marks. Bullets are commonplace in informal writing, although they remain less acceptable in formal venues, such as academic writing.

Used correctly, bullets highlight distinct but *equal* parts of a whole. For example:

Good, not necessarily tenured, professors usually possess three [equally important] qualities:
- They are knowledgeable.
- They are dedicated.
- They are accessible.

Our spy pens come in four colors: [*Or*]   Our spy pens come in four colors:

• black	• black,
• grey	• grey,
• grey and black	• grey and black, and
• black and white	• black and white.

If you have subpoints under a bullet, your second-level bullets must be visually subordinate (i.e., smaller).

Our spy pens come in four colors:
- black
  - black with white gun silhouettes
  - black with green gun silhouettes
  - black with yellow gun silhouettes

The rise of the bullet has also brought overuse and incorrect use. Only the romance challenged, for sure, would ever use bullets to segment a narrative.

- Romeo met Juliet.
- They fell in love.
- Their unenlightened parents didn't approve.
- Romeo and Juliet killed themselves.

Two cautionary points about bullets bear emphasizing:

- Bullets do not magically support or prove anything. They are not a substitute for necessary description, analysis, and interpretation, and they do not replace the evidence and reasoning you would ordinarily be expected to provide. Bullets simply grab and direct the readers' attention by saying, "Look at me." The text following the bullet is what matters.

- Bullets should be used judiciously. Over-bulleting is much like "crying wolf" and expecting your reader to keep paying attention. Bullets should neither highlight every paragraph nor serve as some sort of annoying design element adorning every paragraph. Whole paragraphs can be bulleted when they develop a larger idea/argument to which they are subordinate. In these cases, each bulleted paragraph functions much like an item in a list, but with more elaboration. This paragraph and the previous one illustrate the point.

Use numbers, not bullets, to indicate how a list of items should be ranked or sequenced.

U.S. News & World Report ranked these schools as having the top 2016 Executive MBA programs:[1]

[Without Punctuation]	*[With Punctuation]*
1. University of Pennsylvania	1. University of Pennsylvania,
2. University of Chicago	2. University of Chicago, and
3. Northwestern University	3. Northwestern University.

To assemble this product, follow these steps:

1. connect part A to part B	1. Connect part A to part B.
2. connect part B to part C	2. Connect part B to part C.
3. connect part C to part D	3. Connect part C to part D.

Use numbers instead of bullets for lengthy lists, even if the items are equal, because numbers allow for easier referencing. You would say, *Question 17 restates Question 4*, not *The seventeenth bulleted question restates the fourth bulleted question*. Use numbers also when you want to identify specific items within a paragraphed text, where bullets would not work because they must be vertically positioned to achieve their visual effect. This (1) makes good sense and (2) should be obvious.

Choose a Sensible Typeface

Formatting your message also means choosing an appropriate typeface. Typefaces fall into two major categories: serif and sans-serif. Serif typefaces primarily feature serifs, which are small, tail-like finishing touches on the ends of characters. Sans-serif typefaces do not have serifs. Popular serif typefaces include Baskerville Old Face, Bookman Old Style, Century, Garamond, Georgia, Palatino Linotype, and Times New Roman. Popular sans-serif typefaces include Arial, Calibri, Helvetica, Tahoma, and Verdana. (Optima, the typeface used in this book, is classified as a sans-serif, although it actually melds serif and sans-serif elements to form a design both elegant and easy to read.)

Conventional wisdom, supported generally but not conclusively by research studies, suggests that most serif typefaces are easier to read than sans-serif typefaces in printed text, which accounts for serif's dominant use in printed newspapers, magazines, and books. Sans-serif typefaces, though, are usually easier to read on a computer screen owing to the screen's lower resolution compared to the printed page. In print, sans-serif fonts are fine for headings and short copy. They also work well in PowerPoint and Prezi presentations, where each slide contains but a few lines of text.

Oddly, many writers choose traditional sans-serif typefaces, like Arial, for their printed texts. In the absence of stronger evidence that most sans-serif typefaces are as readable as serif typefaces in hard copy, it is better to stick with the latter. As we become more accustomed to sans-serif

Renovation Tip

James Thurber said, "Don't get it right, just get it written."[2] Finish your entire draft, no matter how rough the copy, before beginning any major rewriting. Fixating over imperfect sentences and paragraphs early in the writing process can interrupt your creative momentum. It is also simpler to revise once you see where all your ideas/arguments fall, which also spares you from reworking material you may end up deleting. On your first draft, include just about everything because, later, cutting will be easier than adding. This allows you to work through your thoughts and revise them more effectively.

typefaces because of their widespread use in digital formats, we may find sans-serif typefaces easier and faster to read in all formats.

The problem of some serif typefaces appearing smaller and "muddier" can be rectified by increasing their point size from 12 to 12.5 or 13. When you do this with Times New Roman, for example, it appears similar in size to 12-point Arial.

The typeface you choose should be well designed for its intended medium. Fortunately, newer serif typefaces (such as Georgia) and sans-serif typefaces (such as Verdana) are continually being developed and improved specifically for the computer screen and the printed page.

Revising How You Revise

Review Your Writing in Both Digital and Printed Forms

Throughout this book, a recurring theme has been that the process of rewriting is enhanced when you create distance between you the writer and you the editor. Previous suggestions for creating this distance have included letting your writing "rest" between revisions to ensure its sense-making does not benefit from your proximity to the text; using a reverse outline to reveal organizational problems you may not routinely detect; and seeing how a potential reader might organize and revise a sample of your writing.

Another way to create critical distance is to review your message in both digital and printed forms. Nearly all of us today type our first draft on a computer, where we also make all or most of our revisions. More experienced writers usually alternate between revising their drafts onscreen and in print. Both approaches have their advantages.

Onscreen revising allows you to quickly try out different versions of the same sentence or paragraph. When you revise your message, the onscreen image instantly reflects the changes. The emerging "clean" text, free of handwritten edits, is visually easier to read, which facilitates more immediate revising. Onscreen word-processing programs also offer dictionaries, thesauruses, and tools for correcting spelling and grammar.

Hard copy revising, on the other hand, distances you more from the original digital form. The mode of presentation (hard copy rather than digital) and the venue (usually somewhere away from your computer) alter your orientation and corresponding critical perspective. For some, it becomes easier to approach the printed draft as if they were the reader, not the writer.

Although computers allow for scrolling and jumping from page to page, it is not quite the same as when your eyes scan a printed text. A manuscript spread across a desk, for example, lets you view multiple paragraphs and pages at once, as well as weave between paragraphs and pages without any of them digitally disappearing. You're able to *see* problems that do not come across as readily on the computer screen. Organizational glitches stand out, as well as problems with topic sentences, unity and coherence, and language repetition.

Critique the Writing of Others

When time allows and friends are willing, invite another set of fresh eyes to review your writing. Because editing someone else's work is much easier than composing your own, nearly everyone, including those having modest writing skills, can provide you with helpful suggestions. If possible, try to solicit and encourage feedback that goes beyond cursory commentary, which, unfortunately, usually becomes the norm because in-depth critique is so labor intensive.

You can also improve your writing and rewriting skills by reviewing the work of others. The process can significantly help you become a better writer, especially if you focus on providing corrective feedback that *shows* how to fix the text. The act of showing—of editing and rewriting—becomes self-instructive.

On the other hand, when feedback reflects only narrative reaction, the critique becomes marginal, both literally and figuratively. Physically confined to the margins of the paper, it takes the form of short, conclusory comments, such as "confusing," "unclear," "elaborate." And it is only marginally helpful: it references problems without illustrating how to remedy them, and it ignores more serious faults relating to organization, unity, and coherence.

Marginal criticism looks like the sample in Box 4.3. By not venturing beyond the margins, the reviewer never *enters* the text to engage in the kind of correction that would most benefit the writer. As opposed to the critique in Box 4.3, a more helpful approach would go deeper in guiding the writer. It would look more like the critique in Box 4.4.

Box 4.3 The Kardashians, Turnitin, and the Ford Motor Company: A Marxist Analysis of the New Business Model

1st ¶ ....

Statistic is misleading.

Watch the wordy phrasing.

State thesis in active voice.

excellent distinction

confusing; revise

2nd ¶ ....

YES!

Interesting argument, but you need to elaborate.

Can you tie this back to your thesis?

unclear

3rd ¶ ....

awkward phrasing

What's your point? Hard to follow where you're going.

I agree.

Box 4.4 *The Kardashians, Turnitin, and the Ford Motor Company: A Marxist Analysis of the New Business Model*

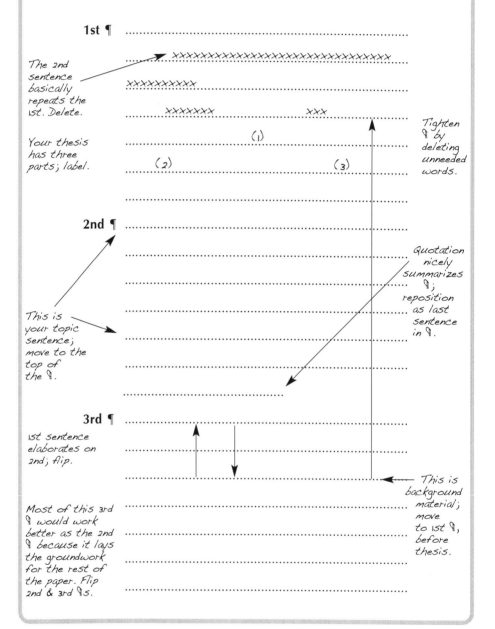

1st ¶

The 2nd sentence basically repeats the 1st. Delete.

Your thesis has three parts; label.

(1)
(2)
(3)

Tighten ¶ by deleting unneeded words.

2nd ¶

This is your topic sentence; move to the top of the ¶.

Quotation nicely summarizes ¶; reposition as last sentence in ¶.

3rd ¶

1st sentence elaborates on 2nd; flip.

This is background material; move to 1st ¶, before thesis.

Most of this 3rd ¶ would work better as the 2nd ¶ because it lays the groundwork for the rest of the paper. Flip 2nd & 3rd ¶s.

Renovation Tip

These additional tips can aid you in completing the revision process:

Read your writing aloud

Because the spoken word is processed differently than the written word, reading your writing aloud provides another way of assessing your message. Speaking your words also underscores the flow (the rhythm and grace) of your writing. Awkward phrases and structures, in particular, stand out orally, as do repetitive word use and sentence patterns.

Format your text for editing

Writers will frequently choose to triple/quadruple space drafts of their work to physically facilitate subsequent revision. Less common is the strategy of cramming as much text as possible onto the page—using single spacing, narrower margins, smaller point type—to visually expose a larger portion of the manuscript at once. This makes it easier to spot linguistic, structural, and ideational repetition, which can otherwise go undetected in a more traditional layout. Published authors know this reality all too well. Often, it is only after viewing their manuscript in page proofs, where repetitive elements *appear* closer together owing to the published page having compressed the text, that they notice the repetition.

Know when you are done

One sign your final revision is nearing completion is when you find yourself changing recent edits back to their previous versions. Should this happen, bring the writing to a close, or, at very least, let your paper rest before returning to its review.

EXERCISES

Exercise 1

Bring to class a lengthy newspaper, magazine, or Web-based article that has not been formatted with headings and subheadings. Exchange selections with a classmate. Format your classmate's selection with headings and, where appropriate, subheadings. Review and discuss how each of you made your formatting decisions. Do your headings and subheadings effectively summarize the sections they cover? Could any be better worded? Are any other headings and subheadings needed?

Exercise 2

Below is a list of summary information about five football games, presented without benefit of visual cues to indicate which content goes together. Where would you insert space breaks to aid the reader's understanding? (Hint: more than one correct answer is possible.)

Alabama Victorious at Home.

The game went into three overtimes before a trick play decided it.

Final Score, 46–45.

Oklahoma Wins by One Point.

The controversial ending came in the closing seconds on a snowy field.

Ohio State Loses Narrowly on Last Play.

A missed extra point led to a 7–6 score.

Northwestern Wins Close One.

Final Score, 28–27.

LSU Takes Game in a Nail Biter.

Exercise 3

Break into small groups and discuss the process by which each of you write and rewrite papers. What approaches and strategies seem to work best and why? From your own writing experiences, what other renovating tips not included in this book would you offer?

Notes

1   "Executive MBA." *U.S. News & World Report*, Sept. 13, 2016, www.usnews. com/best-graduate-schools/top-business-schools/executive-rankings?int=aa6b09 &int=a06908

2   Thurber, James. "Fables for Our Time—IV." *The New Yorker*, April 29, 1939, p. 23.

PART

II

Additional Tools

5 Rating Your Readability

In the 1920s, educators began developing readability formulas as a way of determining suitable reading books for different grade-school levels. They showed how tabulations of word and sentence length could measure writing complexity and thereby predict whether readers would understand what they read. Early readability formulas, however, were too complicated and tedious for everyday use.

In 1944, Robert Gunning developed a simple, quick, and reliable way to measure writing complexity, called the Fog Index[sm] scale.[1] The Fog Index[sm] score[2] represents the approximate number of years of schooling *theoretically* needed to comprehend, with 90 percent or better accuracy, a passage of writing. Texts with lower scores are easier to read and understand than texts with higher scores. Gunning observed that scores above 12 represented difficult reading, and that "almost anything [but not everything] can be written within the easy-reading range."

Fog Index[sm] scores reflect the reading grade level, not the intelligence level, implied by the text. A message written at an 8th grade reading level does not mean it resembles something an eighth-grader would write. Nor does a message having a 16th grade reading level mean that a college graduate wrote it. A sophisticated, well-executed message may have a low Fog Index[sm] score, while a simplistic, clumsily written text may score high. Similarly, a seasoned reader of modest formal education could have less trouble navigating a densely fogged writing sample than might a freshly minted college graduate.

Keep in mind that the Fog Index[sm] scale is a tool, not a prescription, which works best when used from time to time to monitor the complexity of your writing. If your scores are consistently high on everything you compose, take a closer look to see whether all your messages warrant a similar vocabulary and sentence structure.

Finding Your Fog Index^{SM} Score

Pick a writing sample of at least 100 words, ending with a period. Then, follow these steps:

1. **Figure your Average Sentence Length (ASL)**
   Divide the number of words in your sample by the number of sentences. Treat all independent clauses as separate sentences, even when commas or semicolons are used instead of periods to separate them. *We studied, we learned, and we improved* counts as three sentences, as does *We studied; we learned; we improved.* Hyphenated words (twenty-five), numbers (92,748), and dates (2017) count as one word (June 22, 1916 = three words).

2. **Determine your Percentage of Polysyllabic Words (PPW)**
   Count the words of three syllables or more. Do not count capitalized words, including the first word of each sentence, or verbs made into three syllables by adding *-ed* or *-es* (such as *created* or *trespasses*). Divide the number of words of three or more syllables by the word length of your sample. This determines your percentage of polysyllabic words. For example, 16 long words in a 130-word sample equals 12.3%. (To arrive at this percentage, divide 16 by 130 and then press the percentage key; or divide 16 by 130 and multiply the result—0.123— by 100.) Treat this percentage as a whole number when you add it to your average sentence length.

3. **Add your ASL to your PPW and multiply by 0.4.**
   Round up the result to the nearest one-tenth percent.

   Examples:

13.50	ASL (135 words ÷ 10 sentences)
+	
6.67%	PPW (9 polysyllabic words ÷ 135 words)
20.17	
(×) 0.4	
8.068	Fog Index^{sm} score: **8.1**

16.25	ASL (195 words ÷ 12 sentences)
+	
10.77%	PPW (21 polysyllabic words ÷ 195 words)
27.02	
(×) 0.4	
10.808	Fog Index^{sm} score: **10.8**

Fog Index^{sm} scores are useful, but they do not tell the whole story. They measure neither a text's unity nor its coherence. They simply map your word and sentence length, two key ingredients in determining readability. However, as shown earlier, readability is influenced by many other factors, such as how well you develop, structure, and format your message. No matter how short your words and sentences, your message will not be easy to read if it is poorly forged, badly organized, and visually unappealing.

Putting the Fog Index^{SM} Scale to Work

The revisions of the three examples that follow show how their Fog Index^{sm} scores—and their lengths—can be cut.

Example 1

Original Fog Index^{sm} Score: 22.3

A **disposition** toward the **encouragement** and **exercise** of **cogency** in **composition** has prompted **publication** and **distribution** of this book.

19.00	ASL (19 words ÷ 1 sentence)
+	
36.84%	PPW (7 polysyllabic words ÷ 19 words)
55.84	
(×) 0.4	
22.336	Fog Index^{sm} score: **22.3**

Revised Fog Index^{sm} Score: 8.1

The goal of this book is to help you write more **cogently**.

12.00	ASL (12 words ÷ 1 sentence)
+	
8.33%	PPW (1 polysyllabic word ÷ 12 words)
20.33	
(×) 0.4	
8.132	Fog Index^{sm} score: **8.1**

Example 2

Original Fog Index^{sm} Score: 27.2

Despite the fact that the time required for **improving** your writing skills may seem **excessive** at the **beginning**, it will pay **dividends** in the long run **insofar** as once a **reasonable** degree of writing **proficiency** is achieved, it will **appreciably** improve your course grades and **dramatically** enhance your sex appeal.

50.00	ASL (50 words ÷ 1 sentence)
+	
18.00%	PPW (9 polysyllabic words ÷ 50 words)
68.00	
(×) 0.4	
27.20	Fog Index^{sm} score: **27.2**

Revised Fog Index^{sm} Score: 7

At first, it will seem to take **forever** to improve your writing skills. But once you do, it will greatly improve your grades and enhance your sex appeal.

14.00	ASL (28 words ÷ 2 sentences)
+	
3.57%	PPW (1 polysyllabic word ÷ 28 words)
17.57	
(×) 0.4	
7.028	Fog Index^{sm} score: **7**

Example 3

Original Fog Index^sm Score: 17.5

There are any number of **companies** that offer writing workshops that have as their **ultimate** purpose to train **individuals** how to write better. Through one's **attendance** at these workshops, one can achieve an **enhancement** of **personal** writing skills. This is **important** because success in almost any field of **endeavor** can be **accomplished** on a **regular** basis if one writes well.

But **improving** writing skills requires the **willingness** to **undertake** the **commitment** to working hard on one's writing, and, **unfortunately**, the **decision** to confront one's writing **difficulties** is something that many **individuals** won't accept because they **mistakenly** think they **already** write **terrifically**. Consequently, they are not **receptive** to **receiving instruction** in their writing efforts.

22.60	ASL (113 words ÷ 5 sentences)
+	
21.24%	PPW (24 polysyllabic words ÷ 113 words)
43.84	
(×) 0.4	
17.54	Fog Index^sm score: **17.5**

Revised Fog Index^sm Score: 8.1

Many **companies** offer workshops that train people how to write better and thus enhance their job **performance**.

Coupled with hard work, these workshops can improve most people's writing skills. Yet many are not willing to put forth such effort because they don't think their writing needs any help.

16.00	ASL (48 words ÷ 3 sentences)
+	
4.17%	PPW (2 polysyllabic words ÷ 48 words)
20.17	
(×) 0.4	
8.068	Fog Index^sm score: **8.1**

Here is a slightly different, bulleted revision:

Many **companies** offer workshops that train people how to write better and thus enhance their job **performance**. These workshops can improve most people's writing if they will
- first admit their writing needs help, and then
- **continually** work to hone their skills.

10.25	ASL (41 words ÷ 4 sentences)
+	
7.32%	PPW (3 polysyllabic words ÷ 41 words)
17.57	
(×) 0.4	
7.028	Fog Index^{sm} score: **7**

Note: Count each bulleted item, whatever its length, as one sentence. If the bulleted item comprises more than one sentence, count each sentence separately.

A low Fog Index^{sm} score does not always mean your writing is concise any more than a high Fog Index^{sm} score proves the reverse. A Fog Index^{sm} score of 8 is too high if the text is still wordy. And a Fog Index^{sm} score that exceeds 12 is not a problem if the message deals with difficult concepts that could not be expressed as well with shorter words and shorter sentences. One criticism of academic writing is not that the Fog Index^{sm} scores per se are high, which is to be expected given the complexity of the material explored, but that the scores are so much higher than necessary. Good writing in any context remains free of *needless* complexity.

Notes

1   Gunning, Robert. *The Technique of Clear Writing.* McGraw-Hill, 1952.

2   Fog Index^{sm} is a service mark owned by Richard Kallan.

6

Learning to Write Cogently

Novelists and other dramatists have long extolled the practice of nonfiction writing, specifically journalism, as a way of gaining worldly experience, learning information-gathering techniques, and tightening one's prose style. Describing this idealized career path, journalist-turned-novelist Tom Wolfe writes in *The New Journalism*:

> The idea was to get a job on a newspaper, keep body and soul together, pay the rent, get to know "the world," accumulate "experience," perhaps work some of the fat off your style—then, at some point, quit cold, say good-bye to journalism, move into a shack somewhere, work night and day for six months, and light up the sky with the final triumph. The final triumph was known as The Novel.[1]

Just as the practice of nonfiction writing improves one's ability to craft fiction, so, too, it can be argued, does the reverse hold true: the practice of fictive storytelling leads to a more cogent nonfiction writing style.

One unique way of experiencing the benefits of dramatic writing is by composing 55-word short stories. Because the form is so brief, its successful completion mandates the writer's scrutinizing of every word used, as well as the questioning and analyzing of every sentence's function. What is 55-word storytelling, and how can it improve your writing?

History and Structure of Short Fiction

The 55-word short story belongs to a category of brief fiction, ranging in length from 55 words to 1,750 words, which has been called various names, including *short shorts, short short stories, sudden fiction, flash fiction, microfiction,* and *fast fiction.* Such fiction, says Jerome Stern in his 1996 edited volume *Micro Fiction: An Anthology of Really Short Stories,* is "an ancient and honorable form, deeply rooted in the human psyche and in the history of human communities,"[2] whose earlier predecessors include anecdotes, jokes, fables, and parables. Although variations of brief fiction have been around forever, the impetus for contemporary efforts, according to Robert Shapard and James Thomas, who edited the 1986 anthology *Sudden Fiction: American Short-Short Stories,* can be traced to "the spirit of experiment and wordplay in the 1960s."[3] It was then, recalls Stern, that "writers like Russel Edson and Enrique Anderson Imbert started writing stories only a few lines long, as if to pose the question 'Can a short story be too short to be a short story?'"[4] Thus far, it would appear that 55 words is about the minimum length.

To understand the nature and structure of a 55-word story is to first recognize what it is *not.* It is not the familiar soundbite or contracted argument that now floods our airways. Nor is it simply an observation, reflection, perspective, or philosophy on life. All could be found in any story, but none by itself constitutes storytelling. Quite simply, a 55-word story is an exceptionally short story having a beginning, a middle, and an end. But it is more.

In *The World's Shortest Stories,* a 1995 collection of 55-word efforts, editor Steve Moss reminds us that all stories, regardless of length, must contain four elements: character(s), setting, conflict, and resolution. The character(s), or the story's actor(s), can be human, animal, or even inanimate. Setting, where the story takes place, might be anywhere, including the recesses of one's mind. Conflict refers to the overarching tension or struggle that generates and propels the story. Resolution, which completes the story, describes how characters address the conflict; it is the culminating action or nonaction expressed by deeds, words, or thoughts. Boxes 6.1 and 6.2, taken from Moss's collection, exemplify the story form.[5]

Box 6.1 "Bedtime Story" by Jeffrey Whitmore

"Careful, honey, it's loaded," he said, re-entering the bedroom.

Her back rested against the headboard. "This for your wife?"

"No. Too chancy. I'm hiring a professional."

"How about me?"

He smirked. "Cute. But who'd be dumb enough to hire a lady hit man?"

She wet her lips, sighting along the barrel. "Your wife."

Box 6.2 "Like Two Ships" by Chris Macy

He entered the elevator.

"Ground floor, please," he said.

He sounds nice, she thought, but he wouldn't notice me.

He noticed. He noticed her standing there, eyes straight ahead. But he didn't blame her.

Nice perfume, he thought as they parted, he lightly stroking his disfigured face, she counting the steps to the waiting van.

As is true of all quality 55-word storytelling, these two stories develop character, setting, conflict, and resolution quickly and economically. The opening sentence of each provides the setting (a bedroom; an elevator). A sentence or two later, all characters are introduced (a husband and his lover; two strangers). Both tales build swiftly to their conflict: What will happen to the husband's wife? Will the strangers unite? Only when readers reach each story's last line, albeit the last word, does resolution come: the lover is the assassin, but hired by the wife to kill the unfaithful husband; the lovelorn strangers will not couple because they misconstrue the inactions of the other.

The writing of 55-word short stories differs from the authoring of more conventional, protracted literature. Traditional dramatic expressions allow for conceptualizing and "working through" story elements during the writing process, but this is not practical when constructing what customarily amounts to a four- or five-sentence story. Nor is it wise: the structural and stylistic challenges of compressing a story into 55 words are daunting enough without the additional burden of trying to discover one's message (the character[s], setting, conflict, and resolution) along the way.

Fifty-five-word storytelling requires its author to envision the entire story before drafting narrative and dialogue. Extensive prewriting produces the purpose and direction needed to execute a form whose brevity is transcending. Successful 55-word authorship begins by grasping the crux of the story: What will happen and why, or, in other words, what will be the story's resolution and its rationale as developed through character, setting, and conflict?

The writing of 55-word stories teaches you how to manage language effectively and efficiently. The exercise's objective, which is more about advancing a cogent style than developing creative storytelling skills, can also be met by constructing 55-word stories that are *factually* based. Regardless of how the story's "raw data" are secured, the assignment calls for a frugal and precise expression of thought, whose pursuit garners lessons about cogency that the writer experiences firsthand.

Stylistic Characteristics of Short Fiction

Quality 55-word stories tend to be stylistically characterized by

- active verbs;
- concise, minimally modified language;
- short-worded, short sentences;
- reader-inferred detailing; and
- rhythmic style and grace.

These characteristics, most of which also hallmark effective nonfiction writing, repeatedly appear in quality 55-word stories because they represent the only viable responses to the form's constraints.

The very process of creating 55-word stories forces its authors to embrace a plain but powerful verb-oriented style easily accessible to the reader. Consider, for a moment, how the 55-word story encourages the use of active verbs. Only by adopting a simple and direct sentence style can one stay within the assignment's 55-word maximum. Creating active voice constructions, instead of their wordier passive counterparts, becomes a vital, ongoing activity rather than something addressed primarily in final editing. Put another way, the 55-word story compels active voice constructions because it is "peak" driven. Practically, it cannot include any of the typical story "valleys" where passive voice flourishes. In *Writing for Story*, two-time Pulitzer Prize winner Jon Franklin insists that all short stories, whether fictional or factual, are similar.

> As you examine the dramatic rises and falls of a story, the most striking thing is that the valleys, where the images begin to build, are where you find the greatest proportion of passive statements. . . . As the drama builds toward a dramatic crest, the sentence length falls off and the proportion of static verbs drops. . . . As the wave builds . . . [the writer's] latitude diminishes. Now, as ascent becomes steep, the possibility of a misstep increases and the danger grows. Each step, now, carries great risk. . . . Each image must be ever more clear and ever more active.[6]

Because 55-word stories must peak quickly, writing in active voice assumes greater significance, informing the entire text by reshaping how the writer perceives and presents story ideas.

The brevity of the 55-word story invites the use of concise language with minimal adjectival and adverbial modification. And because you must develop conflict and resolution rapidly, an action-reliant style featuring short words and short sentences and leaving reasonable inference to the reader often emerges. "Bedtime Story," for instance, contains 12 sentences having an average length of 4.6 words, while "Like Two Ships" has seven sentences, each averaging 7.9 words. In both stories, "difficult" words (words of three or more syllables, excluding those made into three syllables by adding -*ed* or -*es*), which usually take the form of adjectives and adverbs, account for just 3.6 percent (two words) of each text.

As might be expected, both stories score well on various readability indexes. On the Fog Index[sm] scale, "Bedtime Story" scores a remarkable 3.3, theoretically meaning it is easy enough to be read and understood by a person with only slightly better than a 3rd grade education. "Like Two Ships" scores 4.6.

Quality 55-word stories are also marked by their rhythmic grace. This may surprise those expecting a style dominated by tiny sentences to sound choppy and irritatingly monotonous because it lacks the flow and elegance incurred through artful transition, imagery, and other sentence-extending elaboration. What enables 55-word stories to be different? The answer may rest in the form's solicitation of a tight story structure girded by sentences that follow one another closely and naturally. It is when short sentences do not build upon one another that they seem discrete. The 55-word story affirms that when you carefully assemble and position sentences, regardless of their length, you can create fluid, stylistically snug prose, as seen in Box 6.3.

Box 6.3 *"Student Power" by Richard Kallan*

By far, he was the worst so-called brilliant professor I ever had. Disorganized, unfocused, incoherent. He made little sense.

Outraged, I circulated a petition, got 37 students to sign, and presented it to a shocked dean.

A year later, he worked a reduced teaching load. Sweet victory? Today, he died of a brain tumor.

Although 55-word stories are not characterized stylistically by any specific punctuation, they reward the use of certain marks that students usually under employ. The 55-word story author profits by knowing, for example, that the semicolon can replace the coordinating conjunction between independent clauses, thus saving a word or two, and that the colon can dramatically introduce and emphasize ideas, as well as move the narrative along by facilitating a repetitive structure that eliminates the need for transitional material, exemplified in Box 6.4.

The writer who practices 55-word storytelling in conjunction with learning about punctuation comes to realize that a valuable payoff results from knowing, for example, how to use commas to avoid confusion over meaning, question marks (after rhetorical questions) to drive home a point, dashes to highlight parenthetical thought, and ellipses to save words and indicate pause. Far from hindering creativity, knowing punctuation aids

---

> ## Box 6.4 "What Every Teacher Knows" by Richard Kallan
>
> The essay exam: Only Johnson, Garcia, and Ahmad got A's.
>
> The multiple-choice exam: Only Johnson, Garcia, and Ahmad got A's.
>
> The oral exam: Only Johnson, Garcia, and Ahmad got A's.
>
> The final exam: Took the papers, flung them high in the air, and gave A's to only those that never came down. Three didn't.

the process. "There is no conflict between personal approach and basic rules," says Lajos Egri in *The Art of Dramatic Writing: Its Basis in the Creative Interpretation of Human Motives*. "If you know the principles, you will be a better craftsman and artist."[7]

A Short Conclusion about Short Fiction

The 55-word short story form prompts you to interact with your text in ways you seldom do. You are afforded an immersive exercise that asks you to study, evaluate, and remedy your writing. Continually, you must determine whether your stylistic choices function effectively and efficiently. The experience emphasizes the power, versatility, and richness of language to both inform and persuade. Practitioners begin to recognize the might of cogent expression.

Forcing you to stretch your writing proficiencies and produce concise, tightly structured prose, the 55-word short story exercise proves most beneficial when you struggle with its completion, when you find yourself confronting and critically viewing your writing from every angle in hopes of meeting the challenges of the form. The process makes you a better writer even if you do not finish all your stories. And if somewhere along the way you become so smitten by the lure of fictive prose that you decide to forsake your career and head for that proverbial shack to write the Great American Novel? You, too, will have benefited from the exercise.

Notes

1   Wolfe, Tom. *The New Journalism*, with an anthology edited by Tom Wolfe and E. W. Johnson. Harper and Row, 1973, p. 5.

2   Stern, Jerome, editor. *Micro Fiction: An Anthology of Really Short Stories.* W. W. Norton, 1996, p. 17.

3   Shapard, Robert, and James Thomas, editors. *Sudden Fiction: American Short-Short-Stories.* Gibbs Smith, 1986, p. xiv.

4   Stern, p. 18.

5   From *The World's Shortest Stories*, edited by Steve Moss, copyright © 1998, 1995 by Steve Moss, published by Running Press, pp. 13, 76. Permission courtesy of Daniel & Daniel, Publishers.

6   Franklin, Jon. *Writing for Story: Craft Secrets of Dramatic Nonfiction by a Two-Time Pulitzer Prize Winner.* Penguin, 1986, pp. 185–86.

7   Egri, Lajos. *The Art of Dramatic Writing: Its Basis in the Creative Interpretation of Human Motives.* Simon & Shuster, 1960, p. 265.